100
FAVOURITE POEMS
of the
COUNTRYSIDE

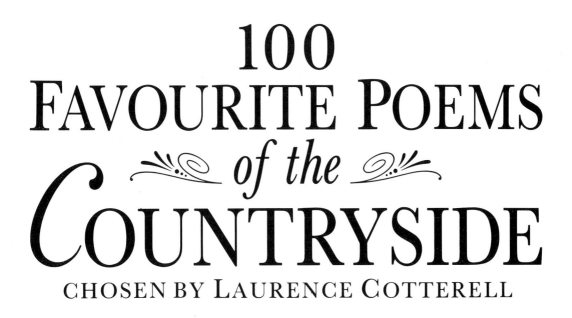

100
FAVOURITE POEMS
of the
COUNTRYSIDE

CHOSEN BY LAURENCE COTTERELL

BCA

LONDON · NEW YORK · SYDNEY · TORONTO

This edition published
1991 by BCA
by arrangement with
Judy Piatkus (Publishers) Ltd

CN 8605

Printed and bound in Great Britain by
Butler & Tanner Ltd, Frome and London

Contents

LIST OF PAINTINGS

INTRODUCTION

As with its forerunner, *100 Favourite Poems*, there has been no problem at all in finding a hundred favourite poems of the countryside – or several hundred for that matter. The problem again has been the whittling down from a huge, varied array of well-known and oft-quoted pieces.

Thus, once more, I turn longevity to good account by calling on memory to select a hundred poems which could be said to be of the countryside in one facet or another – a hundred constantly quoted in print, or quoted frequently enough where people congregate. These are a hundred from among what I judge to be well-loved poems in this genre – not necessarily the Top Hundred in populist order. To have adopted the Top of the Pops principle would have meant fewer poets being represented, and much space being taken up by a comparatively small group.

Not all the verses in this selection relate to the countryside of the British Isles specifically, but most of them do by the nature of things, since we are considering poetry in English. Poetry is the one art form at which the English are supreme, and I make no apology for repeating that when I say 'English' I mean all those, whatever their origins or backgrounds, who use the English language as their means of expression, whether in 'purest' form or adaptation. And my reference to 'the countryside of the British Isles' is deliberate since Irish, Scots and Welsh poets are properly represented. And, looking at lyrical 'countryside' poems in the English language, I could not resist including pieces by the Americans W. Bliss Carman, Emily Dickinson and T. S. Eliot.

Only three living poets are included, not because there is no good, thoughtful verse still being written on country and environmental themes, but only because there has not been time for such works to seep into mass consciousness.

One of those three poems by living writers, *Song at the Beginning of Autumn*, by Elizabeth Jennings, happens to have caught on swiftly with a wide audience, and I can only record as I find. That comment applies even more forcibly to Laurie Lee, whose *April Rise* appears here, and whose works have achieved immense popularity in a relatively short time since *Cider with Rosie*.

The other, *My Land*, by Catherine Cookson, is unique in the context of this selection. It was not published until 1988, when it appeared in Mrs Cookson's 'personal anthology', *Let Me Make Myself Plain*; but because of the author's enormous following this piece is already known to hundreds of thousands. *My Land* also happens to be, in my opinion, true poetry and not mere verse, although that same popularity has almost certainly robbed her of recognition by the poetry reviewers.

The unflagging readership for Izaak Walton's *Compleat Angler* gives *Coridon's Song* (which comes from that book) a rightful place here. In the book, the poem is attributed to 'Jo Chalkhill', but it is widely believed that this was a non-de-plume for Walton himself.

I am not so conceited as to believe that anyone who takes up this volume will necessarily possess its predecessor, *100 Favourite Poems*. But let me assure those who might have bought the earlier selection that they have not been short-changed by the inclusion in *this* anthology of eight pieces that appeared there! As before, I started from scratch and selected the possibilities for *100 Favourite Poems of the Countryside* in their own right, without reference to the earlier book. Those eight were properly included among *100 Favourite Poems* and are properly included here, where they will perhaps be read in a different context.

I have kept longer poems to a minimum, or have selected extracts from them. Some, however, like the Robert Burns and Swinburne inclusions, lose everything if not quoted in full; whereas, although it hurts to attenuate *The Song of the Plow*, the whole text would indeed overflow, while the extract used here is expressive in itself.

Perhaps the Tyndale & Coverdale version of The Psalms is not so widely quoted today, but I've taken poetic licence in including one of their renditions as a refreshing change from the scriptural 'translation' foisted on Anglicans currently, looking as though it were written by literary eunuchs for a congregation of robots.

This kind of anthology comes appropriately at a moment when vandals are grubbing up much of what is left of the Garden of England. The cynic may say that the English countryside was never like the allegedly idealised concept of many of the poets. The answer is much like Turner's when tackled by an earnest lady who declared that she had never seen a sunset like his portrayals. 'Perhaps not, madam,' he replied. 'But wouldn't you like to!' And we would like to see, and have our children see, what is left of the English countryside, before it is irredeemably mutilated by extensions of an obsolete form of transport, leading to the uglifying 'Chunnel' with its appropriately ugly name. We may yet regret the lack of men

> Much like Jack Cade and Butcher Dick
> Of Ashford both, who struck too wild, too soon,
> Before their time was ripe –

Still showing, nonetheless, the teeth
That tunnel moles, upheaving Kentish Rag,
To choke with gold the county's tilth,
Will yet feel in their rumps
As they, like Say, betray the realm
And rucket up the garden of the land.

How you would rend them, Will!
And, God grant, the Globe
In resurrection soon may house
Some play inspired by your great Bastard, Will,
To outflush all the weevil moneybugs
In their own day, and make their names a mock
While men still stand on grass.

The paintings reproduced in this book have been chosen by layfolk (where art is concerned) to try and evoke for other layfolk the general atmosphere of the poems.

LAURENCE COTTERELL
June 1990

IDYLLIC
AND
LYRICAL

Tom O' Bedlam

The moon's my constant mistress,
And the lonely owl my marrow;
    The flaming drake,
    And the night-crow make
Me music to my sorrow.

I know more than Apollo:
For oft, when he lies sleeping,
    I behold the stars
    At mortal wars,
And the rounded welkin weeping.

The moon embraces her shepherd,
And the Queen of Love her warrior;
    While the first does horn
    The stars of the morn,
And the next the heavenly farrier.

With a host of furious fancies,
Whereof I am commander:
    With a burning spear,
    And a horse of air,
To the wilderness I wander.

With a Knight of ghosts and shadows,
I summoned am to Tourney:
    Ten leagues beyond
    The wide world's end;
Methinks it is no journey.

ANON

Evensong

THRUSH, sing clear, for the spring is here:
Sing, for the summer is near, is near,

All day long thou hast plied thy song,
Hardly hid from the hurrying throng:

Now the shade of the trees is laid
Down the meadow and up the glade:

Now when the air grows cool and rare
Birds of the cloister fall to prayer:

Here is the bed of the patient dead,
Shoulder by shoulder, head by head.

Sweet bells swing in the tower, and ring
Men to worship before their King.

See they come as the grave bells hum,
Restless voices awhile are dumb:

More and more on the sacred floor,
Feet that linger about the door:

Sweet sounds swim through the vaulting dim,
Psalm and canticle, vesper hymn.

That is the way that mortals pray:
Which is the sweeter? brown bird, say!

Which were best for me? both are blest;
Sing thy sweetest and leave the rest.

ARTHUR CHRISTOPHER BENSON (1862–1925)

Pippa's Song

THE year's at the spring,
And day's at the morn;
Morning's at seven;
The hill-side's dew-pearl'd;
The lark's on the wing;
The snail's on the thorn;
God's in His heaven –
All's right with the world!

ROBERT BROWNING (1812–1889)

In Romney Marsh

As I went down to Dymchurch Wall,
 I heard the South sing o'er the land;
I saw the yellow sunlight fall
 On knolls where Norman churches stand.

And ringing shrilly, taut and lithe,
 Within the wind a core of sound,
The wire from Romney town to Hythe
 Alone its airy journey wound.

A veil of purple vapour flowed
 And trailed its fringe along the Straits;
The upper air like sapphire glowed;
 And roses filled Heaven's central gates.

Masts in the offing wagged their tops;
 The swinging waves pealed on the shore;
The saffron beach, all diamond drops
 And beads of surge, prolonged the roar.

As I came up from Dymchurch Wall,
    I saw above the Downs' low crest
The crimson brands of sunset fall,
    Flicker and fade from out the west.

Night sank: like flakes of silver fire
    The stars in one great shower came down;
Shrill blew the wind; and shrill the wire
    Rang out from Hythe to Romney town.

The darkly shining salt sea drops
    Streamed as the waves clashed on the shore;
The beach, with all its organ stops
    Pealing again, prolonged the roar.

JOHN DAVIDSON (1857–1909)

Landscapes

I New Hampshire

CHILDREN'S voices in the orchard
Between the blossom- and the fruit-time:
Golden head, crimson head,
Between the green tip and the root.
Black wing, brown wing, hover over;
Twenty years and the spring is over;
To-day grieves, to-morrow grieves,
Cover me over, light-in-leaves;
Golden head, black wing,
Cling, swing,
Spring, sing,
Swing up into the apple-tree.

II Virginia

Red river, red river,
Slow flow heat is silence
No will is still as a river
Still. Will heat move
Only through the mocking-bird
Heard once? Still hills
Wait. Gates wait. Purple trees,
White trees, wait, wait,
Delay, decay. Living, living,
Never moving. Ever moving
Iron thoughts came with me
And go with me:
Red river, river, river.

T. S. ELIOT (1888–1965)

Oberon's Feast

SHAPCOT! to thee the Fairy State
I with discretion, dedicate.
Because thou prizest things that are
Curious and unfamiliar,
Take first the feast; these dishes gone,
We'll see the Fairy Court anon.
A little mushroom-table spread,
After short prayers, they set on bread;
A moon-parch'd grain of purest wheat,
With some small glittering grit, to eat
His choice bits with; then in a trice
They make a feast less great than nice.
But all this while his eye is serv'd,
We must not think his ear was starv'd
But that there was in place to stir
His spleen, the chirring Grasshopper,
The merry Cricket, puling Fly,
The piping Gnat for minstrelsy.
And now, we must imagine first,
The Elves present to quench his thirst
A pure seed-pearl of infant dew,
Brought and besweetened in a blue
And pregnant violet; which done,
His kitling eyes begin to run
Quite through the table, where he spies
The horns of papery Butterflies:
Of which he eats, and tastes a little
Of that we call the cuckoo's spittle.
A little fuzz-ball pudding stands
By, yet not blessed by his hands,
That was too coarse; but then forthwith
He ventures boldly on the pith
Of sugared rush, and eats the sag
And well bestrutted Bee's sweet bag:
Gladding his palate with some store
Of Emit's eggs; what would he more?

Richard Painton (fl. early 20th century) *The Fairy Queen*, Fine-Lines, Warwickshire

Claude Monet (1840–1926) *The Poppy Field* (detail), Musée d'Orsay, Paris

But beards of Mice, a Newt's stew'd thigh,
A roasted Earwig, and a Fly;
With the red-capp'd Worm, that's shut
Within the concave of a nut,
Brown as his tooth. A little Moth,
Late flattened in a piece of cloth:
With wither'd cherries; Mandrake's ears;
Mole's eyes; to these, the slain Stag's tears;
The unctuous dewlaps of a Snail;
The broke heart of a Nightingale
O'ercome in music; with a wine,
Ne'er ravish'd from the flattering vine,
But gently press'd from the soft side
Of the most sweet and dainty bride,
Brought in a dainty daisy, which
He fully quaffs up to bewitch
His blood to height; this done, commended
Grace by his Priest: *The feast is ended.*

ROBERT HERRICK (1591–1674)

The Wind in a Frolic

THE wind one morning sprang up from sleep,
Saying, 'Now for a frolic! now for a leap!
Now for a mad-cap galloping chase!
I'll make a commotion in every place!'

So it swept with a bustle right through a great town,
Cracking the signs and scattering down
Shutters; and whisking, with merciless squalls,
Old women's bonnets and gingerbread stalls.
There never was heard a much lustier shout,
As the apples and oranges trundled about;
And the urchins that stand with their thievish eyes
For ever on watch ran off each with a prize.

Then away to the fields it went blustering and humming,
And the cattle all wondered what monster was coming.
It plucked by the tails the grave matronly cows.
And tossed the colts' manes all over their brows;
Till, offended at such an unusual salute,
They all turned their backs, and stood sulky and mute.

So on it went, capering and playing its pranks,
Whistling with reeds on the broad river's banks,
Puffing the birds as they sat on the spray,
Or the traveller grave on the King's highway.
Through the forest it roared, and cried gaily, 'Now,
You sturdy old oaks, I'll make you bow!'
And it made them bow without much more ado,
For it cracked their great branches through and through.

Then it rushed like a monster on cottage and farm,
Striking their dwellers with sudden alarm;
And they ran out like bees in a mid-summer swarm:
There were dames with their kerchiefs tied over their caps,
To see if their poultry were free from mishaps;
The turkeys they gobbled, the geese screamed aloud,
And the hens crept to roost in a terrified crowd;
There was rearing of ladders, and logs were laid on,
Where the thatch from the roof threatened soon to be gone.
But the wind had swept on, and had met in a lane
With a schoolboy, who panted and struggled in vain;
For it tossed him and twirled him, then passed — and he stood
With his hat in a pool and his shoes in the mud!

Then away went the wind in its holiday glee,
And now it was far on the billowy sea,
And the lordly ships felt the staggering blow,
And the little boats darted to and fro.
But, lo! it was night, and it sank to rest
On the sea-bird's rock in the gleaming west,
Laughing to think, in its fearful fun,
How little of mischief it really had done.

WILLIAM HOWITT (1729–1879)

From: *L'Allegro*

HASTE thee nymph, and bring with thee
Jest and youthful Jollity,
Quips and Cranks, and wanton Wiles,
Nods, and Becks, and Wreathed Smiles,
Such as hang on *Hebe's* cheek,
And love to live in dimple sleek;
Sport that wrincled Care derides,
And Laughter holding both his sides.
Com, and trip it as ye go
On the light fantastick toe,
And in thy right hand lead with thee,
The Mountain Nymph, sweet Liberty;
And if I give thee honour due,
Mirth, admit me of thy crue
To live with her, and live with thee,
In unreproved pleasures free;
To hear the Lark begin his flight,
And singing startle the dull night,
From his watch-towre in the skies,
Till the dappled dawn doth rise;
Then to com in spight of sorrow,
And at my window bid good morrow,
Through the Sweet-Briar, or the Vine,
Or the twisted Eglantine.
While the Cock with lively din,
Scatters the rear of darknes thin,
And to the stack, or the Barn dore,
Stoutly struts his Dames before,
Oft list'ning how the Hounds and horn,
Clearly rouse the slumbring morn,
From the side of som Hoar Hill,
Through the high wood echoing shrill.
Som time walking not unseen
By Hedge-row Elms, on Hillocks green,
Right against the Eastern gate,
Where the great Sun begins his state,

Rob'd in flames, and Amber light,
The clouds in thousand Liveries dight,
While the Plowman neer at hand,
Whistles ore the Furrow'd Land,
And the Milkmaid singeth blithe,
And the Mower whets his sithe,
And every Shepherd tells his tale
Under the Hawthorn in the dale.
Streit mine eye hath caught new pleasures
Whilst the Lantskip round it measures,
Russet Lawns, and Fallows Gray,
Where the nibling flocks do stray,
Mountains on whose barren brest
The labouring clouds do often rest:
Meadows trim with Daisies pide,
Shallow Brooks, and Rivers wide.
Towers, and Battlements it sees
Boosom'd high in tufted Trees,
Where perhaps som beauty lies,
The Cynosure of neighbouring eyes.
Hard by, a Cottage chimney smokes,
From betwixt two aged Okes,
Where *Corydon* and *Thyrsis* met,
Are at their savory dinner set
Of Hearbs, and other Country Messes,
Which the neat-handed *Phillis* dresses;
And then in haste her Bowre she leaves,
With *Thestylis* to bind the Sheaves;
Or if the earlier season lead
To the tann'd Haycock in the Mead,
Som times with secure delight
The up-land Hamlets will invite,
When the merry Bells ring round,
And the jocond rebecks sound
To many a youth, and many a maid,
Dancing in the Chequer'd shade;
And young and old com forth to play
On a Sunshine Holyday,
Till the live-long day-light fail,

Then to the Spicy Nut-brown Ale,
With stories told of many a feat,
How *Faery Mab* the junkets eat,
She was pincht, and pull'd she sed,
And he by Friars Lanthorn led
Tells how the drudging *Goblin* swet,
To ern his Creame-bowle duly set,
When in one night, ere glimps of morn,
His shadowy Flale hath thresh'd the Corn
That ten day-labourers could not end,
Then lies him down the Lubbar Fend[1],
And stretch'd out all the Chimney's length,
Basks at the fire his hairy strength;
And Crop-full out of dores he flings,
Ere the first Cock his Mattin rings.
Thus don the Tales, to bed they creep,
By whispering Windes soon lull'd asleep.

JOHN MILTON (1608–1674)

[1] a beneficent goblin (fiend) who works at night

In a Meadow

THIS is the place
Where far from the unholy populace
The daughter of Philosophy and Sleep
 Her court doth keep,
Sweet Contemplation. To her service bound
 Hover around
The little amiable summer airs,
 Her courtiers.

 The deep black soil
Makes mute her palace-floors with thick trefoil;
The grasses sagely nodding overhead
 Curtain her bed;
And lest the feet of strangers overpass
 Her walls of grass,
Gravely a little river goes his rounds
 To beat the bounds.

 – No bustling flood
To make a tumult in her neighbourhood,
But such a stream as knows to go and come
 Discreetly dumb.
Therein are chambers tapestried with weeds
 And screen'd with reeds;
For roof the waterlily-leaves serene
 Spread tiles of green.

 The sun's large eye
Falls soberly upon me where I lie;
For delicate webs of immaterial haze
 Refine his rays.
The air is full of music none knows what,
 Or half-forgot;
The living echo of dead voices fills
 The unseen hills.

I hear the song
Of cuckoo answering cuckoo all day long;
And know not if it be my inward sprite
For my delight
Making remember'd poetry appear
As sound in the ear:
Like a salt savour poignant in the breeze
From distant seas.

Dreams without sleep,
And sleep too clear for dreaming and too deep;
And Quiet very large and manifold
About me roll'd;
Satiety, that momentary flower,
Stretch'd to an hour;
These are her gifts which all mankind may use,
And all refuse.

JOHN SWINNERTON PHILLIMORE (1873–1926)

Upon Eckington Bridge,
River Avon

O PASTORAL heart of England! like a psalm
   Of green days telling with a quiet beat –
O wave into the sunset flowing calm!
   O tirèd lark descending on the wheat!
Lies it all peace beyond that western fold
   Where now the lingering shepherd sees his star
Rise upon Malvern?   Paints an Age of Gold
      Yon cloud with prophecies of linkèd ease –
      Lulling this Land, with hills drawn up like knees,
   To drowse beside her implements of war?

Man shall outlast his battles.   They have swept
   Avon from Naseby Field to Severn Ham;
And Evesham's dedicated stones have stepp'd
   Down to the dust with Montfort's oriflame.
Nor the red tear nor the reflected tower
   Abides; but yet these eloquent grooves remain,
Worn in the sandstone parapet hour by hour
      By labouring bargemen where they shifted ropes.
      E'en so shall man turn back from violent hopes
   To Adam's cheer, and toil with spade again.

Ay, and his mother Nature, to whose lap
   Like a repentant child at length he hies,
Not in the whirlwind or the thunder-clap
   Proclaims her more tremendous mysteries:
But when in winter's grave, bereft of light,
   With still, small voice divinelier whispering
– Lifting the green head of the aconite,
      Feeding with sap of hope the hazel-shoot –
      She feels God's finger active at the root,
   Turns in her sleep, and murmurs of the Spring.

SIR ARTHUR QUILLER-COUCH (1863–1944)

Ode to the West Wind

O wild West Wind, thou breath of Autumn's being,
Thou, from whose unseen presence the leaves dead
Are driven, like ghosts from an enchanter fleeing,

Yellow, and black, and pale, and hectic red,
Pestilence-stricken multitudes: O thou,
Who chariotest to their dark wintry bed

The wingèd seeds, where they lie cold and low,
Each like a corpse within its grave, until
Thine azure sister of the Spring shall blow

Her clarion o'er the dreaming earth, and fill
(Driving sweet buds like flocks to feed in air)
With living hues and odours plain and hill:

Wild Spirit, which art moving everywhere;
Destroyer and preserver; hear, oh, hear!

Thou on whose streams, mid the steep sky's commotion,
Loose clouds like earth's decaying leaves are shed,
Shook from the tangled boughs of Heaven and Ocean,

Angels of rain and lightning: there are spread
On the blue surface of thine aëry surge,
Like the bright hair uplifted from the head

Of some fierce Maenad, even from the dim verge
Of the horizon to the zenith's height,
The locks of the approaching storm. Thou dirge

Of the dying year, to which this closing night
Will be the dome of a vast sepulchre,
Vaulted with all thy congregated might

Of vapours, from whose solid atmosphere
Black rain, and fire, and hail will burst: oh, hear!

Thou who didst waken from his summer dreams
The blue Mediterranean, where he lay,
Lulled by the coil of his crystàlline streams,

Beside a pumice isle in Baiae's bay,
And saw in sleep old palaces and towers
Quivering within the wave's intenser day,

All overgrown with azure moss and flowers
So sweet, the sense faints picturing them! Thou
For whose path the Atlantic's level powers

Cleave themselves into chasms, while far below
The sea-blooms and the oozy woods which wear
The sapless foliage of the ocean, know

Thy voice, and suddenly grow gray with fear,
And tremble and despoil themselves: oh, hear!

If I were a dead leaf thou mightest bear;
If I were a swift cloud to fly with thee;
A wave to pant beneath thy power, and share

The impulse of thy strength, only less free
Than thou, O uncontrollable! If even
I were as in my boyhood, and could be

The comrade of thy wanderings over Heaven,
As then, when to outstrip thy skiey speed
Scarce seemed a vision; I would ne'er have striven

As thus with thee in prayer in my sore need.
Oh, lift me as a wave, a leaf, a cloud!
I fall upon the thorns of life! I bleed!
A heavy weight of hours has chained and bowed
One too like thee: tameless, and swift, and proud.

Make me thy lyre, even as the forest is:
What if my leaves are falling like its own!
The tumult of thy mighty harmonies

Will take from both a deep, autumnal tone,
Sweet though in sadness. Be thou, Spirit fierce,
My spirit! Be thou me, impetuous one!

Drive my dead thoughts over the universe
Like withered leaves to quicken a new birth!
And, by the incantation of this verse,

Scatter, as from an unextinguished hearth
Ashes and sparks, my words among mankind!
Be through my lips to unawakened earth

The trumpet of a prophecy! O, Wind,
If Winter comes, can Spring be far behind?

PERCY BYSSHE SHELLEY (1792–1822)

The Comforters

WHEN I crept over the hill, broken with tears,
    When I crouched down on the grass, dumb in despair,
I heard the soft croon of the wind bend to my ears,
    I felt the light kiss of the wind touching my hair.

When I stood lone on the height my sorrow did speak,
    As I went down the hill, I cried and I cried,
The soft little hands of the rain stroking my cheek,
    The kind little feet of the rain ran by my side.

When I went to thy grave, broken with tears,
    When I crouched down in the grass, dumb in despair,
I heard the sweet croon of the wind soft in my ears,
    I felt the kind lips of the wind touching my hair.

When I stood lone by thy cross, sorrow did speak.
    When I went down the long hill, I cried and I cried.
The soft little hands of the rain stroked my pale cheek,
    The kind little feet of the rain ran by my side.

DORA SIGERSON SHORTER (1870–1918)

Song from The Brook

I COME from haunts of coot and hern,
 I make a sudden sally
And sparkle out among the fern,
 To bicker down a valley.

By thirty hills I hurry down,
 Or slip between the ridges,
By twenty thorps, a little town,
 And half a hundred bridges.

Till last by Philip's farm I flow
 To join the brimming river,
For men may come and men may go,
 But I go on for ever.

*   *   *

I chatter over stony ways,
 In little sharps and trebles,
I bubble into eddying bays,
 I babble on the pebbles.

With many a curve my banks I fret
 By many a field and fallow,
And many a fairy foreland set
 With willow-weed and mallow.

I chatter, chatter, as I flow
 To join the brimming river,
For men may come and men may go,
 But I go on for ever.

*   *   *

I wind about, and in and out,
    With here a blossom sailing,
And here and there a lusty trout,
    And here and there a grayling,

And here and there a foamy flake
    Upon me, as I travel
With many a silvery waterbreak
    Above the golden gravel,

And draw them all along, and flow
    To join the brimming river,
For men may come and men may go,
    But I go on for ever.

ALFRED, LORD TENNYSON (1809–1892)

Fern Hill

Now as I was young and easy under the apple boughs
About the lilting house and happy as the grass was green,
　　The night above the dingle starry,
　　　　Time let me hail and climb
　　Golden in the heydays of his eyes,
And honoured among the wagons I was prince of the apple towns
And once below a time I lordly had the trees and leaves
　　　　Trail with daisies and barley
　　Down the rivers of the windfall light.

And as I was green and carefree, famous among the barns
About the happy yard and singing as the farm was home,
　　In the sun that is young once only,
　　　　Time let me play and be
　　Golden in the mercy of his means,
And green and golden I was huntsman and herdsman, the calves
Sang to my horn, the foxes on the hills barked clear and cold,
　　　　And the sabbath rang slowly
　　In the pebbles of the holy streams.

All the sun long it was running, it was lovely, the hay
Fields high as the house, the tunes from the chimneys, it was air
　　And playing, lovely and watery
　　　　And fire green as grass.
　　And nightly under the simple stars
As I rode to sleep the owls were bearing the farm away,
All the moon long I heard, blessed among stables, the nightjars
　　Flying with the ricks, and the horses
　　　　Flashing into the dark.

Claude Monet (1840–1926) *Women in the Garden*, Musée d'Orsay, Paris

Charles Robertson (1844–1891) *By the River*, Guildford House Gallery, Surrey

And then to awake, and the farm, like a wanderer white
With the dew, come back, the cock on his shoulder: it was all
    Shining, it was Adam and maiden,
        The sky gathered again
    And the sun grew round that very day.
So it must have been after the birth of the simple light
In the first, spinning place, the spellbound horses walking warm
    Out of the whinnying green stable
        On to the fields of praise.

And honoured among foxes and pheasants by the gay house
Under the new made clouds and happy as the heart was long,
    In the sun born over and over,
        I ran my heedless ways,
    My wishes raced through the house high hay
And nothing I cared, at my sky blue trades, that time allows
In all his tuneful turning so few and such morning songs
    Before the children green and golden
        Follow him out of grace,

Nothing I cared, in the lamb white days, that time would take me
Up to the swallow thronged loft by the shadow of my hand,
    In the moon that is always rising,
        Nor that riding to sleep
    I should hear him fly with the high fields
And wake to the farm forever fled from the childless land.
Oh as I was young and easy in the mercy of his means,
        Time held me green and dying
    Though I sang in my chains like the sea.

DYLAN THOMAS (1914–1953)

Scents

To-day I think
Only with scents, – scents dead leaves yield,
And bracken, and wild carrot's seed,
And the square mustard field;

Odours that rise
When the spade wounds the root of tree,
Rose, currant, raspberry, or goutweed,
Rhubarb or celery;

The smoke's smell, too,
Flowing from where a bonfire burns
The dead, the waste, the dangerous,
And all to sweetness turns.

It is enough
To smell, to crumble the dark earth,
While the robin sings over again
Sad songs of Autumn mirth.

EDWARD THOMAS (1878–1917)

CONSERVATION
AND
DEPREDATION

Middlesex

GAILY into Ruislip Gardens
    Runs the red electric train,
With a thousand Ta's and Pardon's
    Daintily alights Elaine;
Hurries down the concrete station
With a frown of concentration,
Out into the outskirt's edges
Where a few surviving hedges
Keep alive our lost Elysium – rural Middlesex again.

Well cut Windsmoor flapping lightly,
    Jacqmar scarf of mauve and green
Hiding hair which, Friday nightly,
    Delicately drowns in Drene;
Fair Elaine the bobby-soxer,
Fresh-complexioned with Innoxa,
Gains the garden – father's hobby –
Hangs her Windsmoor in the lobby,
Settles down to sandwich supper and the television screen.

Gentle Brent, I used to know you
    Wandering Wembley-wards at will,
Now what change your waters show you
    In the meadowlands you fill!
Recollect the elm-trees misty
And the footpaths climbing twisty
Under cedar-shaded palings,
Low laburnum-leaned-on railings,
Out of Northolt on and upward to the heights of Harrow hill.

Parish of enormous hayfields
    Perivale stood all alone,
And from Greenford scent of mayfields
    Most enticingly was blown
Over market gardens tidy,
Taverns for the *bona fide*,
Cockney anglers, cockney shooters,
    Murray Poshes, Lupin-Pooters
Long in Kensal Green and Highgate silent under soot and stone.

SIR JOHN BETJEMAN (1906–1984)

To Ironfounders and Others

WHEN you destroy a blade of grass
You poison England at her roots:
Remember no man's foot can pass
Where evermore no green life shoots.

You force the birds to wing too high
Where your unnatural vapours creep:
Surely the living rocks shall die
When birds no rightful distance keep.

You have brought down the firmament
And yet no heaven is more near;
You shape huge deeds without event,
And half-made men believe and fear.

Your worship is your furnaces,
Which, like old idols, lost obscenes,
Have molten bowels; your vision is
Machines for making more machines.

O, you are buried in the night,
Preparing destinies of rust;
Iron misused must turn to blight
And dwindle to a tetter'd crust.

The grass, forerunner of life, has gone,
But plants that spring in ruins and shards
Attend until your dream is done:
I have seen hemlock in your yards.

The generations of the worm
Know not your loads piled on their soil;
Their knotted ganglions shall wax firm
Till your strong flagstones heave and toil.

When the old hollow'd earth is crack'd
And when, to grasp more power and feasts,
Its ores are emptied, wasted, lack'd
The middens of your burning beasts

Shall be raked over till they yield
Last priceless slags for fashionings high,
Ploughs to wake grass in every field,
Chisels men's hands to magnify.

GORDON BOTTOMLEY (1874–1948)

From: *The Deserted Village*

Sᴡᴇᴇᴛ Auburn! loveliest village of the plain,
Where health and plenty cheer'd the labouring swain,
Where smiling spring its earliest visit paid,
And parting summer's lingering blooms delay'd:
Dear lovely bowers of innocence and ease,
Seats of my youth, when every sport could please:
How often have I loiter'd o'er thy green,
Where humble happiness endear'd each scene!
How often have I paused on every charm,
The shelter'd cot, the cultivated farm,
The never failing brook, the busy mill,
The decent church that topp'd the neighbouring hill,
The hawthorn bush, with seats beneath the shade,
For talking age and whispering lovers made!
How often have I bless'd the coming day,
When toil remitting lent its turn to play,
And all the village train, from labour free,
Led up their sports beneath the spreading tree:
While many a pastime circled in the shade,
The young contending as the old survey'd;
And many a gambol frolick'd o'er the ground,
And slights of art and feats of strength went round.
And still, as each repeated pleasure tired,
Succeeding sports the mirthful band inspired;
The dancing pair that simply sought renown,
By holding out to tire each other down;
The swain mistrustless of his smutted face,
While secret laughter titter'd round the place;
The bashful virgin's sidelong looks of love,
The matron's glance that would those looks reprove.
These were thy charms, sweet village! sports like these,
With sweet succession, taught e'en toil to please;
These round thy bowers their cheerful influence shed,
These were thy charms – but all these charms are fled.
    Sweet smiling village, loveliest of the lawn,
Thy sports are fled, and all thy charms withdrawn;

Amidst thy bowers the tyrant's hand is seen,
And desolation saddens all thy green:
One only master grasps the whole domain,
And half a tillage stints thy smiling plain;
No more thy glassy brook reflects the day,
But choked with sedges works its weedy way;
Along thy glades, a solitary guest,
The hollow-sounding bittern guards its nest;
Amidst thy desert walks the lapwing flies,
And tires their echoes with unvaried cries.
Sunk are thy bowers in shapeless ruin all,
And the long grass o'ertops the mouldering wall;
And, trembling, shrinking from the spoiler's hand
Far, far away thy children leave the land.

Ill fares the land, to hastening ills a prey,
Where wealth accumulates, and men decay;
Princes and lords may flourish or may fade;
A breath can make them, as a breath has made:
But a bold peasantry, their country's pride,
When once destroy'd, can never be supplied.

A time there was, ere England's griefs began,
When every rood of ground maintained its man;
For him light labour spread her wholesome store,
Just gave what life required, but gave no more:
His best companions, innocence and health;
And his best riches, ignorance of wealth.

But times are altered; trade's unfeeling train
Usurp the land and dispossess the swain;
Along the lawn, where scattered hamlets rose,
Unwieldy wealth, and cumbrous pomp repose;
And every want to oppulence allied,
And every pang that folly pays to pride.
These gentle hours that plenty bade to bloom,
Those calm desires that asked but little room,
Those healthful sports that graced the peaceful scene,
Lived in each look, and brightened all the green;
These far departing seek a kinder shore,
And rural mirth and manners are no more.

OLIVER GOLDSMITH (1728–1774)

From: *The Song of the Plow*

The Outlook

O WHAT see you from your gray hill?
The sun is low, the air all gold,
Warm lies the slumbrous land and still.
I see the river with deep and shallow,
I see the ford, I hear the mill;
I see the cattle upon the fallow;
    And there the manor half in trees,
    And there the church and the acre hallow
Where lie your dead in their feretories
    Of clay and dust and crumble of peat,
    With a stone or two to their memories:
Your dead who with their sweat kept sweet
    This heritage of gray and green,
    This England now the richer for it.
I see the yews and the thatch between,
    The smoke that tells of cottage and hearth,
    And all as it has ever been
From the beginning on this old earth.
    And so it is even as it was
    From the beginning in Hodge's garth,
While kings and statesmen flaunt and pass,
    Kings and lords and knights of the shire,
    Bishops in lawn (rare flesh to be grass!),
Priest and schoolman, clerk and esquire;
    Danes and Normans and Scottishmen,
    Frenchmen, Brunswickers, son after sire,
They come and conquer, they ruffle and reign,
    They rule, they rise, they spend, they grudge,
    They bicker their threescore years and ten,

They slay, and thieve, and go; but Hodge
   The Englishman stoops to fork and flail,
And serves Saint Use, and will not budge,

Saint Use

But drives the furrow and fills the pail,
   Raining sweat lest the land go dry:
   He sees his masters, he gives them hail
With hand to forelock as they ride by —
   They that eat what he doth bake,
   They that hold what he must buy,
   They that spend what he doth make,
     They that are rich by other men's toil;
     They of the sword and he of the rake,
The lords of the land, the son of the soil!
   O Christ, the Patron of the Poor,
   Thou who didst suffer harlot's oil
Anoint Thy feet, O narrow Door!
   Thou who didst sanctify our dearth
   With bitter pain and anguish sore,
A barefoot King held nothing worth —
   Here's misery for Thy chrism to mend:
   A thousand years to plow the earth,
And be worse off at journey's end!

MAURICE HEWLETT (1861–1923)

I Remember, I Remember

I REMEMBER, I remember
The house where I was born,
The little window where the sun
Came peeping in at morn;
He never came a wink too soon
Nor brought too long a day;
But now, I often wish the night
Had borne my breath away.

I remember, I remember
The roses, red and white,
The violets, and the lily-cups —
Those flowers made of light!
The lilacs where the robin built,
And where my brother set
The laburnum on his birth-day, —
The tree is living yet!

I remember, I remember
Where I was used to swing,
And thought the air must rush as fresh
To swallows on the wing;
My spirit flew in feathers then
That is so heavy now,
And summer pools could hardly cool
The fever on my brow.

I remember, I remember
The fir trees dark and high;
I used to think their slender tops
Were close against the sky:
It was a childish ignorance,
But now 'tis little joy
To know I'm farther off from Heaven
Than when I was a boy.

THOMAS HOOD (1799–1845)

The Plough

A Landscape in Berkshire

ABOVE yon sombre swell of land
    Thou see'st the dawn's grave orange hue,
With one pale streak like yellow sand,
    And over that a vein of blue.

The air is cold above the woods;
    All silent is the earth and sky,
Except with his own lonely moods
    The blackbird holds a colloquy.

Over the broad hill creeps a beam,
    Like hope that gilds a good man's brow;
And now ascends the nostril-stream
    Of stalwart horses come to plough.

Ye rigid Ploughmen, bear in mind
    Your labour is for future hours:
Advance – spare not – nor look behind –
    Plough deep and straight with all your powers!

R. H. HORNE (1803–1884)

The Roadside Fire

I WILL make you brooches and toys for your delight
Of bird-song at morning and star-shine at night.
I will make a palace fit for you and me,
Of green days in forests and blue days at sea.

I will make my kitchen, and you shall keep your room,
Where white flows the river and bright blows the broom,
And you shall wash your linen and keep your body white
In rainfall at morning and dewfall at night.

And this shall be for music when no one else is near,
The fine song for singing, the rare song to hear!
That only I remember, that only you admire,
Of the broad road that stretches and the roadside fire.

ROBERT LOUIS STEVENSON (1850–1894)

A Forsaken Garden

IN a coign of the cliff between lowland and highland,
    At the sea-down's edge between windward and lee,
Walled round with rocks as an inland island,
    The ghost of a garden fronts the sea.
A girdle of brushwood and thorn encloses
    The steep square slope of the blossomless bed
Where the weeds that grew green from the graves of its roses
            Now lie dead.

The fields fall southward, abrupt and broken,
    To the low last edge of the long lone land.
If a step should sound or a word be spoken,
    Would a ghost not rise at the strange guest's hand?
So long have the grey bare walks lain guestless,
    Through branches and briars if a man make way,
He shall find no life but the sea-wind's, restless
            Night and day.

The dense hard passage is blind and stifled
 That crawls by a track none turn to climb
To the strait waste place that the years have rifled
 Of all but the thorns that are touched not of time.
The thorns he spares when the rose is taken;
 The rocks are left when he wastes the plain.
The wind that wanders, the weeds wind-shaken,
   These remain.

Not a flower to be pressed of the foot that falls not;
 As the heart of a dead man the seed-plots are dry;
From the thicket of thorns whence the nightingale calls not,
 Could she call, there were never a rose to reply.
Over the meadows that blossom and wither
 Rings but the note of a sea-bird's song;
Only the sun and the rain come hither
   All year long.

The sun burns sere and the rain dishevels
 One gaunt bleak blossom of scentless breach.
Only the wind here hovers and revels
 In a round where life seems barren as death.
Here there was laughing of old, there was weeping,
 Haply, of lovers none ever will know,
Whose eyes went seaward a hundred sleeping
   Years ago.

Heart handfast in heart as they stood, 'Look thither,'
 Did he whisper? 'look forth from the flowers to the sea;
For the foam-flowers endure when the rose-blossoms wither,
 And men that love lightly may die — but we?'
And the same wind sang and the same waves whitened,
 And or ever the garden's last petals were shed,
In the lips that had whispered, the eyes that had lightened,
   Love was dead.

Or they loved their life through, and then went whither?
    And were one to the end – but what end who knows?
Love deep as the sea as a rose must wither,
    As the rose-red seaweed that mocks the rose.
Shall the dead take thought for the dead to love them?
    What love was ever as deep as a grave?
They are loveless now as the grass above them
        Or the wave.

All are at one now, roses and lovers,
    Not known of the cliffs and the fields and the sea.
Not a breath of the time that has been hovers
    In the air now soft with a summer to be.
Not a breath shall there sweeten the seasons hereafter
    Of the flowers or the lovers that laugh now or weep,
When as they that are free now of weeping and laughter
        We shall sleep.

Here death may deal not again for ever;
    Here change may come not till all change end.
From the graves they have made they shall rise up never,
    Who have left nought living to ravage and rend.
Earth, stones, and thorns of the wild ground growing,
    While the sun and the rain live, these shall be;
Till a last wind's breath upon all these blowing
        Roll the sea.

Till the slow sea rise and the sheer cliff crumble,
    Till terrace and meadow the deep gulfs drink,
Till the strength of the waves of the high tides humble
    The fields that lessen, the rocks that shrink,
Here now in his triumph where all things falter,
    Stretched out on the spoils that his own hand spread,
As a god self-slain on his own strange altar,
        Death lies dead.

ALGERNON CHARLES SWINBURNE (1837–1909)

PURELY PASTORAL

George Cole (1810–1883) *Pastoral Scene*, Roy Miles Fine Paintings, London

John Constable (1776–1837) *The Haywain* (detail), National Gallery, London

Amid the Barren Hills

THERE is a spot, 'mid barren hills,
   Where winter howls, and driving rain;
But, if the dreary tempest chills,
   There is a light that warms again.

The house is old, the trees are bare,
   Moonless above bends twilight's dome;
But what on earth is half so dear –
   So longed for – as the hearth of home?

The mute bird sitting on the stone,
   The dank moss dripping from the wall,
The thorn-trees gaunt, the walks o'ergrown,
   I love them – how I love them all! . . .

A little and a lone green lane
   That opened on a common wide;
A distant, dreamy, dim blue chain
   Of mountains, circling every side.

A heaven so clear, an earth so calm,
   So sweet, so soft, so hushed an air;
And, deepening still the dream-like charm,
   Wild moor-sheep feeding everywhere.

EMILY BRONTE (1818–1848)

From: *Aurora Leigh*

The Sweetness of Engand

Whoever lives true life, will love true love.
I learnt to love that England. Very oft,
Before the day was born, or otherwise
Through secret windings of the afternoons,
I threw my hunters off and plunged myself
Among the deep hills, as a hunted stag
Will take the waters, shivering with the fear
And passion of the course. And when at last
Escaped, so many a green slope built on slope
Betwixt me and the enemy's house behind,
I dared to rest, or wander, in a rest
Made sweeter for the step upon the grass,
And view the ground's most gentle dimplement
(As if God's finger touched but did not press
In making England), such an up and down
Of verdure, – nothing too much up or down,
A ripple of land; such little hills, the sky
Can stoop to tenderly and the wheat-fields climb;
Such nooks of valleys lined with orchises,
Fed full of noises by invisible streams;
And open pastures where you scarcely tell
White daisies from white dew, – at intervals
The mythic oaks and elm-trees standing out
Self-poised upon their prodigy of shade, –
I thought my father's land was worthy too
Of being my Shakespeare's.

*   *   *

But then the thrushes sang,
And shook my pulses and the elms' new leaves;
At which I turned, and held my finger up,
And bade him mark that, howsoe'er the world
Went ill, as he related, certainly
The thrushes still sang in it. At the word
His brow would soften, – and he bore with me
In melancholy patience, not unkind,
While breaking into voluble ecstasy

I flattered all the beauteous country round,
As poets use, the skies, the clouds, the fields,
The happy violets hiding from the roads
The primroses run down to, carrying gold;
The tangled hedgerows, where the cows push out
Impatient horns and tolerant churning mouths
'Twixt dripping ash-boughs, – hedgerows all alive
With birds and gnats and large white butterflies
Which look as if the May-flower had caught life
And palpitated forth upon the wind;
Hills, vales, woods, netted in a silver mist,
Farms, granges, doubled up among the hills;
And cattle grazing in the watered vales,
And cottage-chimneys smoking from the woods,
And cottage-gardens smelling everywhere,
Confused with smell of orchards.

ELIZABETH BARRETT BROWNING (1806–1861)

A Musical Instrument

WHAT was he doing, the great god Pan,
    Down in the reeds by the river?
Spreading ruin and scattering ban,
Splashing and paddling with hoofs of a goat,
And breaking the golden lilies afloat
    With the dragon-fly on the river.

He tore out a reed, the great god Pan,
    From the deep cool bed of the river;
The limpid water turbidly ran,
And the broken lilies a-dying lay,
And the dragon-fly had fled away,
    Ere he brought it out of the river.

High on the shore sat the great god Pan,
    While turbidly flow'd the river;
And hack'd and hew'd as a great god can
With his hard bleak steel at the patient reed,
Till there was not a sign of the leaf indeed
    To prove it fresh from the river.

He cut it short, did the great god Pan
    (How tall it stood in the river!),
Then drew the pith, like the heart of a man,
Steadily from the outside ring,
And notch'd the poor dry empty thing
    In holes, as he sat by the river.

'This is the way,' laugh'd the great god Pan
    (Laugh'd as he sat by the river),
'The only way since gods began
To make sweet music they could succeed.'
Then dropping his mouth to a hole in the reed,
    He blew in power by the river.

Sweet, sweet, sweet, O Pan!
    Piercing sweet by the river!
Blinding sweet, O great god Pan!
The sun on the hill forgot to die,
And the lilies revived, and the dragon-fly
    Came back to dream on the river.

Yet half a beast is the great god Pan,
    To laugh as he sits by the river,
Making a poet out of a man:
The true gods sigh for the cost and pain —
For the reed which grows nevermore again
    As a reed with the reeds of the river.

ELIZABETH BARRETT BROWNING (1806–1861)

In the Heart of the Hills

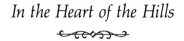

In the warm blue heart of the hills
    My beautiful beautiful one
Sleeps where he laid him down
    Before the journey was done.

All the long summer day
    The ghosts of noon draw nigh,
And the tremulous aspens hear
    The footing of winds go by.

Down to the gates of the sea,
    Out of the gates of the west,
Journeys the whispering river
    Before the place of his rest.

The road he loved to follow
    When June came by his door,
Out through the dim blue haze
    Leads, but allures no more.

The trailing shadows of clouds
    Steal from the slopes and are gone:
The myriad life in the grass
    Stirs, but he slumbers on;

The inland-wandering tern
    Skriel as they forage and fly;
His loons on the lonely reach
    Utter their querulous cry;

Over the floating lilies
    A dragon-fly tacks and steers;
Far in the depth of the blue
    A martin settles and veers;

To every roadside thistle
  A gold-brown butterfly clings;
But he no more companions
  All the dear vagrant things.

The strong red journeying sun,
  The pale and wandering rain,
Will roam on the hills together
  And find him never again.

Then twilight falls with the touch
  Of a hand that soothes and stills,
And a swamp-robin sings into light
  The lone white star of the hills.

Alone in the dusk he sings,
  And a burden of sorrow and wrong
Is lifted up from the earth
  And carried away in his song.

Alone in the dusk he sings,
  And the joy of another day
Is folded in peace and borne
  On the drift of years away.

But there in the heart of the hills
  My beautiful weary one
Sleeps where I laid him down;
  And the long sweet night is begun.

W. BLISS CARMAN (1861–1929)

My Land

My land of deep lakes
With mountain shadows
Like ancient cities
Buried and at rest in their depths;
My land of hidden valleys
Dotted with homesteads,
Solitary, aloof;
My land of barren fells,
Scree slopes gripped by hooves of sheep
And rams protective of their own;
My land of skies stretching to infinity,
Blue high sheets of sheer clear light;
My land of mists,
Grey, wet, body-soaking mists
That shroud you to a trembling halt;
My land of tones
Fan-lit and sombre,
Heather purples and autumn golds;
Winter white,
Black frost laden nights
Driving hard to spring
And new born grass
And released water
Rushing from its prison of ice.
Oh, my land of sturdy men,
Short, stumpy in part,
And women warm of heart
And worth
And laughing lips,
My land of the North.

CATHERINE COOKSON (1906–   )

The Song of Favonius

THE flagon topped with foaming ale
Invokes the song and faery tale,
And he who sings the sweetest song
To him the flagon shall belong,
The silver flagon richly chased
With hops and barley interlaced;
But he who tells the fairest tale
More than the singer shall prevail,
For he shall win the prize divine,
The fragrant kiss of Proserpine.

The sweetest singer we will lead
In triumph down the river mead,
There lightly brushing with our knees
Through gold and purple irises
Until we reach the spearmint mound,
Where he with bay-leaves shall be crowned.
But he who tells the fairest tale
More than the singer shall prevail,
For he shall win the prize divine,
The fragrant kiss of Proserpine.

A song of love is sweet to hear,
And sweet the song of merry cheer;
So may the muses ever find
True votaries among mankind
In taverns and in maidens' bowers,
In Winter and in Summer hours.
But he who tells the fairest tale
More than the singer shall prevail,
For he shall win the prize divine,
The fragrant kiss of Proserpine.

And he shall be the king, and wear
The muses' circle on his hair,
The magic coronal of old,
The coronal of faery gold;
And triumph over Pluto gain
Where Chaucer, Keats and Morris reign.
The flagon topped with foaming ale
Invokes the song and faery tale.
Now who will win the prize divine,
The fragrant kiss of Proserpine?

CHARLES DALMON (1872–1938)

A Narrow Fellow
in the Grass

A NARROW fellow in the grass
Occasionally rides;
You may have met him, – did you not?
His notice sudden is.

The grass divides as with a comb,
A spotted shaft is seen;
And then it closes at your feet
And opens further on.

He likes a boggy acre,
A floor too cool for corn.
Yet when a child, and barefoot,
I more than once, at morn,

Have passed, I thought, a whip-lash
Upbraiding in the sun, –
When, stooping to secure it,
It wrinkled, and was gone.

Several of nature's people
I know, and they know me;
I feel for them a transport
Of cordiality;

But never met this fellow,
Attended or alone,
Without a tighter breathing,
And zero at the bone.

EMILY DICKINSON (1830–1886)

The Feathers
of the Willow

THE feathers of the willow
Are half of them grown yellow
   Above the swelling stream;
And ragged are the bushes,
And rusty now the rushes,
   And wild the clouded gleam.

The thistle now is older,
His stalk begins to moulder,
   His head is white as snow;
The branches all are barer,
The linnet's song is rarer,
   The robin pipeth now.

R. WATSON DIXON (1833–1900)

The Little Waves of Breffny

THE grand road from the mountain goes shining to the sea,
    And there is traffic in it, and many a horse and cart,
But the little roads of Cloonagh are dearer far to me,
    And the little roads of Cloonagh go rambling through
        my heart.
A great storm from the ocean goes shouting o'er
    And there is glory in it and terror on the wind,
But the haunted air of twilight is very strange and still,
    And the little winds of twilight are dearer to my mind.

The great waves of the Atlantic sweep storming on their
        way,
    Shining green and silver with the hidden herring shoal;
But the Little Waves of Breffny have drenched my heart
        in spray,
    And the Little Waves of Breffny go stumbling through
        my soul.

EVA GORE-BOOTH (1870–1926)

Lying in the Grass

BETWEEN two golden tufts of summer grass,
I see the world through hot air as through glass,
And by my face sweet lights and colours pass.

Before me, dark against the fading sky,
I watch three mowers mowing, as I lie:
With brawny arms they sweep in harmony.

Brown English faces by the sun burnt red,
Rich glowing colour on bare throat and head,
My heart would leap to watch them, were I dead!

And in my strong young living as I lie,
I seem to move with them in harmony, –
A fourth is mowing, and that fourth am I.

The music of the scythes that glide and leap,
The young men whistling as their great arms sweep,
And all the perfume and sweet sense of sleep,

The weary butterflies that droop their wings,
The dreamy nightingale that hardly sings,
And all the lassitude of happy things,

Is mingling with the warm and pulsing blood
That gushes through my veins a languid flood,
And feeds my spirit as the sap a bud.

Behind the mowers, on the amber air,
A dark-green beech-wood rises, still and fair,
A white path winding up it like a stair.

And see that girl, with pitcher on her head,
And clean white apron on her gown of red, –
Her even-song of love is but half-said:

She waits the youngest mower.   Now he goes:
Her cheeks are redder than a wild blush-rose:
They climb up where the deepest shadows close.

But though they pass, and vanish, I am there;
I watch his rough hands meet beneath her hair,
Their broken speech sounds sweet to me like prayer.

Ah! now the rosy children come to play,
And romp and struggle with the new-mown hay;
Their clear high voices sound from far away.

They know so little why the world is sad,
They dig themselves warm graves and yet are glad;
Their muffled screams and laughter make me mad!

I long to go and play among them there;
Unseen, like wind, to take them by the hair,
And gently make their rosy cheeks more fair.

The happy children! full of frank surprise,
And sudden whims and innocent ecstasies;
What godhead sparkles from their liquid eyes!

No wonder round those urns of mingled clays
That Tuscan potters fashioned in old days,
And coloured like the torrid earth ablaze,

We find the little gods and loves portrayed,
Through ancient forests wandering undismayed,
And fluting hymns of pleasure unafraid.

They knew, as I do now, what keen delight,
A strong man feels to watch the tender flight
Of little children playing in his sight;

What pure sweet pleasure, and what sacred love,
Comes drifting down upon us from above,
In watching how their limbs and features move.

I do not hunger for a well-stored mind,
I only wish to live my life, and find
My heart in unison with all mankind.

My life is like the single dewy star
That trembles on the horizon's primrose-bar, —
A microcosm where all things living are.

And if, among the noiseless grasses, Death
Should come behind and take away my breath,
I should not rise as one who sorroweth;

For I should pass, but all the world would be
Full of desire and young delight and glee,
And why should men be sad through loss of me?

The light is flying; in the silver-blue
The young moon shines from her bright window through:
The mowers all are gone, and I go too.

EDMUND GOSSE (1849–1928)

Charles Edward Wilson (1864–1949) *Feeding the Ducks*, Abbey Antiques, Hemel Hempstead, Herts

Helen Allingham (1848–1926) *Bluebells*, Private Collection

Pied Beauty

Glory be to God for dappled things –
　　For skies of couple-colour as a brinded cow;
　　　　For rose-moles all in stipple upon trout that swim;
Fresh-firecoal chestnut-falls; finches' wings;
　　Landscape plotted and pieced – fold, fallow, and plough;
　　　　And, áll trádes, their gear and tackle and trim.

All things counter, original, spare, strange;
　　Whatever is fickle, freckled (who knows how?)
　　　　With swift, slow; sweet, sour; adazzle, dim;
He fathers-forth whose beauty is past change:
　　　　　　Praise him.

GERARD MANLEY HOPKINS (1844–1889)

Up on the Downs

Up on the downs the red-eyed kestrels hover,
Eyeing the grass.
The field-mouse flits like a shadow into cover
As their shadows pass.

Men are burning the gorse on the down's shoulder;
A drift of smoke
Glitters with fire and hangs, and the skies smoulder,
And the lungs choke.

Once the tribe did thus on the downs, on those downs burning
Men in the frame,
Crying to the gods of the downs till their brains were turning
And the gods came.

And to-day on the downs, in the wind, the hawks, the grasses,
In blood and air,
Something passes me and cries as it passes,
On the chalk downland bare.

JOHN MASEFIELD (1878–1967)

'He Sendeth the Springs
into the Rivers'

HE sendeth the springs into the rivers
Which run among the hills.
All beasts of the field drink thereof
And the wild asses quench their thirst.
Beside them shall the fowls of the air have their habitation
And sing among the branches.
He watereth the hills from above –
The earth is filled with the fruit of thy works.
He bringeth forth grass for the cattle
And green herb for the service of men;
That he may bring food out of the earth and wine that
    maketh glad the heart of man
And oil to make him a cheerful countenance and bread
    to strengthen man's heart.
The trees of the Lord also are full of sap –
Even the cedars of Libanus which he hath planted
Wherein the birds make their nests
And the fir-trees are a dwelling for the stork.
The high hills are a refuge for the wild goats,
And so are the stony rocks for the conies.
He appointed the moon for certain seasons,
And the sun knoweth his going down.
Thou makest darkness that it may be night
Wherein all the beasts of the forest do move.
The lions roaring after their prey
Do seek their meat from God.
The sun ariseth, and they get them away together
And lay them down in their dens.
Man goeth forth to his work, and to his labour
Until the evening.
O Lord, how manifold are thy works!
In wisdom hast thou made them all –
The earth is full of thy riches.

FROM: THE PSALMS
Tyndale and Coverdale version

Song: *Brignal Banks*

(*from Rokeby*)

O, BRIGNAL banks are wild and fair,
    And Greta woods are green,
And you may gather garlands there
    Would grace a summer queen.

And as I rode by Dalton-hall
    Beneath the turrets high,
A maiden on the castle wall
    Was singing merrily, –
'O, Brignal banks are fresh and fair,
    And Great woods are green;
I'd rather rove with Edmund there
    Than reign our English queen.'

'If, maiden, thou wouldst wend with me,
    To leave both tower and town,
Thou first must guess what life lead we,
    That dwell by dale and down.
And if thou canst that riddle read,
    As read full well ye may,
Then to the greenwood shalt thou speed,
    As blithe as Queen of May.'
Yet sung she, 'Brignal banks are fair,
    And Greta woods are green;
I'd rather rove with Edmund there
    Than reign our English queen ...'

SIR WALTER SCOTT (1771–1832)

The Lake Isle of Innisfree

I WILL arise and go now, and go to Innisfree,
And a small cabin build there, of clay and wattles made;
Nine bean rows will I have there, a hive for the honey-bee,
And live alone in the bee-loud glade.

And I shall have some peace there, for peace comes dropping
    slow,
Dropping from the veils of the morning to where the cricket
    sings;
There midnight's all a glimmer, and noon a purple glow,
And evening full of the linnet's wings.

I will arise and go now, for always night and day
I hear lake water lapping with low sounds by the shore;
While I stand on the roadway, or on the pavements grey,
I hear it in the deep heart's core.

W. B. YEATS (1865–1939)

FLORA
AND
FAUNA

White Foxglove

WHITE foxglove, by an angle in the wall,
Secluded, tall,
No vulgar bees
Consult you, wondering
If such a dainty thing
Can give them ease.
Yet what was that?　Sudden a breeze
From the far moorland sighed,
And you replied,
Quiv'ring a moment with a thrill
Sweet, but ineffable.

Was it a kiss that sought you from the bowers
Of happier flowers,
And did not heed
Accessible loveliness,
And with a quaint distress
Hinted the need,
And paused and trembled for its deed,
And so you trembled, too,
No roseate hue
Revealing how the alarmèd sense
Blushed quick – intense?

Ah me!
Such kisses are for roses in the prime,
For braid of lime,
For full-blown blooms,
For ardent breaths outpoured
Obvious, or treasure stored
In honied rooms
Of rare delight, in which the looms
Of nature still conspire
To sate desire.
Not such are you beside the wall,
Cloistered and virginal.

'Twas your wild purple sisters there that passed
Unseen, and cast
The spell.   They hold
The vantage of the heights,
And in you they have rights,
And they are bold:
They know not ever to be cold
Or coy, but they would play
With you alway.
Wherefore their little sprites a-wing
Make onslaught from the ling.

So spake I to the foxglove in my mood,
But was not understood.
Rather she shrank, and in a tenfold whiteness
Condemned what must have seemed to her my lightness.

THOMAS EDWARD BROWN (1830–1897)

From: *The Blackbird*

THE Blackbird has a thousand whims
In choosing places for her nest
In spots that so unlikely seems
As want of skill and hardly taste
Upon the bindings of the hedge
On water grains of high oak tree
In roots oer looked by kecks and sedge
On thorns where every eye may see

Sweet russet stranger welcome here
& may the mirth be long
How sweet at autumns closing year
To hear thy undersong
While on the garden bench I rest
Beneath the eldern leaves
And hear my little merry guest
Sing to the falling leaves

Thy unknown song how sweet to meet
By him who musing walks alone
Though humble hearts thy music greets
Tis not less sweet for being unknown
The far famed nightingale that shares
Praise in but every song
The popular voice of music heirs
& does thy anthem wrong

Tis wrong that thou shouldst be despised
When these gay queens appear
They sing when summer flowers are prized
Thou at the closing year
Well let the heedless and the proud
Vaunt more exalted lays
The joy that thou from sorrow finds
Is more to thee than praise.

JOHN CLARE (1793–1864)

Hares at Play

THE birds are gone to bed the cows are still
And sheep lie panting on each old mole hill
And underneath the willows grey-green bough
Like toil a resting – lies the fallow plough
The timid hares throw daylights fears away
On the lanes road to dust and dance and play
Then dabble in the grain by nought deterred
To lick the dewfall from the barleys beard
Then out they sturt again and round the hill
Like happy thoughts dance squat and loiter still
Till milking maidens in the early morn
Gingle their yokes and start them in the corn
Through well known beaten paths each nimbling hare
Sturts quick as fear – and seeks its hidden lair.

JOHN CLARE (1793–1864)

A Fancy from Fontenelle

THE Rose in the garden slipped her bud,
And she laughed in the pride of her youthful blood
As she thought of the Gardener standing by –
'He is old – so old! And he soon must die!'

The full Rose waxed in the warm June air,
And she spread and spread till her heart lay bare;
And she laughed once more as she heard his tread –
'He is older now! He will soon be dead!'

But the breeze of the morning blew, and found
That the leaves of the blown Rose strewed the ground;
And he came at noon, that Gardener old,
And he raked them gently under the mould.

And I wove the thing to a random rhyme,
For the Rose is Beauty, the Gardener, Time.

AUSTIN DOBSON (1840–1921)

Ducks

I

FROM troubles of the world
I turn to ducks,
Beautiful comical things
Sleeping or curled
Their heads beneath white wings
By water cool,
Or finding curious things
To eat in various mucks
Beneath the pool,
Tails uppermost, or waddling
Sailor-like on the shores
Of ponds, or paddling
– Left! right! – with fanlike feet
Which are for steady oars
When they (white galleys) float
Each bird a boat
Rippling at will the sweet
Wide waterway....
When night is fallen *you* creep
Upstairs, but drakes and dillies
Nest with pale water-stars,
Moonbeams and shadow bars,
And water-lilies:
Fearful too much to sleep
Since they've no locks
To click against the teeth
Of weasel and fox.
And warm beneath
Are eggs of cloudy green
Whence hungry rats and lean
Would stealthily suck
New life, but for the mien,
The bold ferocious mien
Of the mother-duck.

II

Yes, ducks are valiant things
On nests of twigs and straws,
And ducks are soothy things
And lovely on the lake
When that the sunlight draws
Thereon their pictures dim
In colours cool.
And when beneath the pool
They dabble, and when they swim
And make their rippling rings,
O ducks are beautiful things!

But ducks are comical things: —
As comical as you.
Quack!
They waddle round, they do.
They eat all sorts of things.
And then they quack.
By barn and stable and stack
They wander at their will,
But if you go too near
They look at you through black
Small topaz-tinted eyes
And wish you ill.
Triangular and clear
They leave their curious track
In mud at the water's edge,
And there amid the sedge
And slime they gobble and peer
Saying 'Quack! quack!'

III

When God had finished·the stars and whirl of coloured suns
He turned His mind from big things to fashion little ones,
Beautiful tiny things (like daisies) He made, and then
He made the comical ones in case the minds of men
     Should stiffen and become
     Dull, humourless and glum,
And so forgetful of their Maker be
As to take even themselves – *quite seriously.*
Caterpillars and cats are lively and excellent puns;
All God's jokes are good – even the practical ones!
And as for the duck, I think God must have smiled a bit
Seeing those eyes blink on the day He fashioned it.
And He's probably laughing still
         at the sound that came out of its bill!

F. W. HARVEY (1888–1957)

To Daffodils

FAIR daffodils, we weep to see
 You haste away so soon;
As yet the early-rising Sun
 Has not attain'd his noon.
 Stay, stay
 Until the hasting day
 Has run
 But to the even song;
And, having pray'd together, we
 Will go with you along.

We have short time to stay, as you,
 We have as short a Spring;
As quick a growth to meet decay,
 As you, or anything.
 We die
 As your hours do, and dry
 Away
 Like to the Summer's rain;
Or as the pearls of morning's dew,
 Ne'er to be found again.

ROBERT HERRICK (1591–1674)

Sicilian Cyclamens

WHEN he pushed his brush of black hair off his brow:
When she lifted her mop from her eyes, and screwed it in a
    knob behind
        − O act of fearful temerity!
When they felt their foreheads bare, naked to heaven, their
    eyes revealed:
When they felt the light of heaven brandished like a knife
    at their defenceless eyes,
And the sea like a blade at their face,
Mediterranean savages:
When they came out, face-revealed, under heaven, from the
    shaggy undergrowth of their own hair
For the first time,
They saw tiny rose cyclamens between their toes, growing
Where the slow toads sat brooding on the past.

Slow toads, and cyclamen leaves
Stickily glistening with eternal shadow
Keeping to earth.
Cyclamen leaves
Toad-filmy, earth-iridescent
Beautiful
Frost-filigreed
Spumed with mud
Snail-nacreous
Low down.

The shaking aspect of the sea
And man's defenceless bare face
And cyclamens putting their ears back.
Long, pensive, slim-muzzled greyhound buds
Dreamy, not yet present,
Drawn out of earth
At his toes.
Dawn-rose
Sub-delighted, stone-engendered

Sir George Clausen (1852–1944) *Ploughing* (detail), Aberdeen Art Gallery & Museum

Lucien Pissarro (1863–1944) *Les Dindons*, City of Bristol Museum and Art Gallery

Cyclamens, young cyclamens
Arching
Waking, pricking their ears
Like delicate, very-young greyhound bitches
Half-yawning at the open, inexperienced
Vista of day,
Folding back their soundless petalled ears.

Greyhound bitches
Bending their rosy muzzles pensive down,
And breathing soft, unwilling to wake to the new day
Yet sub-delighted.

Ah Mediterranean morning, when our world began!
Far-off Mediterranean mornings,
Pelasgic faces uncovered,
And budding cyclamens.

The hare suddenly goes uphill
Laying back her long ears with unwinking bliss.

And up the pallid, sea-blenched Mediterranean stone slopes
Rose cyclamen, ecstatic fore-runner!
Cyclamens, ruddy-muzzled cyclamens
In little bunches like bunches of wild hares
Muzzled together, ears-aprick,
Whispering witchcraft
Like women at a well, the dawn-fountain.

Greece, and the world's morning
Where all the Parthenon marbles still fostered the roofs of
        the cyclamen.

Violets
Pagan, rosy-muzzled violets
Autumnal,
Dawn-pink,
Dawn-pale
Among squat toad-leaves sprinkling the unborn
Erechtheion marbles.

D. H. LAWRENCE (1885–1930)

The Rose and the Wind

Dawn

THE ROSE

When think you comes the Wind,
The Wind that kisses me and is so kind?
Lo, how the Lily sleeps! her sleep is light;
Would I were like the Lily, pale and white!
Will the Wind come?

THE BEECH

Perchance for thee too soon.

THE ROSE

If not, how could I live until the noon?
What, think you, Beech-tree, makes the Wind delay?
Why comes he not at breaking of the day?

THE BEECH

Hush, child, and, like the Lily, go to sleep.

THE ROSE

You know I cannot.

THE BEECH

Nay, then, do not weep.
(*After a pause*)
Thy lover comes, be happy now, O Rose!
He softly through my bending branches goes.
Soon he shall come, and you shall feel his kiss.

THE ROSE

Already my flushed heart grows faint with bliss;
Love, I have longed for thee through all the night.

THE WIND

And I to kiss thy petals warm and bright.

THE ROSE

Laugh round me, Love, and kiss me; it is well.
Nay, have no fear; the Lily will not tell.

Morning

THE ROSE

'Twas dawn when first you came; and now the sun
Shines brightly, and the dews of dawn are done.
'Tis well you take me so in your embrace,
But lay me back again into my place,
For I am worn, perhaps with bliss extreme.

THE WIND

Nay, you must wake, Love, from this childish dream.

THE ROSE

'Tis thou, Love, seemest changed; thy laugh is loud,
And 'neath thy stormy kiss my head is bowed.
O Love, O Wind, a space wilt thou not spare?

THE WIND

Not while thy petals are so soft and fair!

THE ROSE

My buds are blind with leaves, they cannot see.
O Love, O Wind, wilt thou not pity me?

Evening

THE BEECH

O Wind! a word with you before you pass:
What did you to the Rose, that on the grass
Broken she lies, and pale, who loved you so?

THE WIND

Roses must live and love, and winds must blow.

P. BOURKE MARSTON (1850–1887)

Thistledown

This might have been a place for sleep
But, as from that small hollow there
Hosts of bright thistledown begin
Their dazzling journey through the air,
An idle man can only stare.

They grip their withered edge of stalk
In brief excitement for the wind;
They hold a breathless final talk,
And when their filmy cables part
One almost hears a little cry.

Some cling together while they wait
And droop and gaze and hesitate,
But others leap along the sky,
Or circle round and calmly choose
The gust they know they ought to use.

While some in loving pairs will glide,
Or watch the others as they pass,
Or rest on flowers in the grass,
Or circle through the shining day
Like silvery butterflies at play.

Some catch themselves to every mound,
Then lingeringly and slowly move
As if they knew the precious ground
Were opening for their fertile love:
They almost try to dig, they need
So much to plant their thistle-seed.

HAROLD MONRO (1879–1932)

Twilight Calm

Oh pleasant eventide!
Clouds on the western side
Grow grey and greyer, hiding the warm sun:
The bees and birds, their happy labours done,
    Seek their close nests and bide.

Screened in the leafy wood
The stock-doves sit and brood:
The very squirrel leaps from bough to bough
But lazily; pauses; and settles now
    Where once he stored his food.

One by one the flowers close,
Lily and dewy rose
Shutting their tender petals from the moon:
The grasshoppers are still; but not so soon
    Are still the noisy crows....

From far the lowings come
Of cattle driven home:
From farther still the wind brings fitfully
The vast continual murmur of the sea,
    Now loud, now almost dumb....

Remote, each single star
Comes out, till there they are
All shining brightly. How the dews fall damp!
While close at hand the glow-worm lights her lamp,
    Or twinkles from afar.

But evening now is done
As much as if the sun
Day-giving had arisen in the East —
For night has come; and the great calm has ceased,
    The quiet sands have run.

CHRISTINA ROSSETTI (1830–1894)

From: *A Midsummer Night's Dream*

I KNOW a bank whereon the wild thyme blows,
Where ox-lips and the nodding violet grows;
Quite over-canopied with lush woodbine,
With sweet musk-roses, and with eglantine:
There sleeps Titania some time of the night,
Lull'd in these flowers with dances and delight;
And there the snake throws her enamell'd skin,
Weed wide enough to wrap a fairy in.

WILLIAM SHAKESPEARE (1564–1616)

To a Skylark

HAIL to thee, blithe Spirit!
Bird thou never wert,
That from heaven, or near it,
Pourest thy full heart
In profuse strains of unpremeditated art.

Higher still and higher
From the earth thou springest
Like a cloud of fire;
The blue deep thou wingest,
And singing still dost soar, and soaring ever singest.

In the golden lightning
Of the sunken sun,
O'er which clouds are bright'ning
Thou dost float and run;
Like an unbodied joy whose race is just begun.

The pale purple even
　　Melts around thy flight;
Like a star of heaven,
　　In the broad daylight
Thou art unseen, but yet I hear thy shrill delight:

Keen as are the arrows
　　Of that silver sphere,
Whose intense lamp narrows
　　In the white dawn clear
Until we hardly see – we feel that it is there.

All the earth and air
　　With thy voice is loud,
As, when night is bare,
　　From one lonely cloud
The moon rains out her beams, and heaven is overflowed.

What thou art we know not;
　　What is most like thee?
From rainbow clouds there flow not
　　Drops so bright to see
From thy presence showers a rain of melody.

Like a poet hidden
　　In the light of thought,
Singing hymns unbidden,
　　Till the world is wrought
To sympathy with hopes and fears it heeded not:

Like a high-born maiden
　　In a palace tower,
Soothing her love-laden
　　Soul in secret hour
With music sweet as love, which overflows her bower:

Like a glow-worm golden
　　In a dell of dew,
Scattering unbeholden
　　Its aëreal hue
Among the flowers and grass, which screen it from the view:

Like a rose embowered
In its own green leaves,
By warm winds deflowered,
Till the scent it gives
Goes faint with too much sweet these heavy-wingèd thieves:

Sound of vernal showers
On the twinkling grass,
Rain-awakened flowers,
All that ever was
Joyous, and clear, and fresh, thy music doth surpass:

Teach us, sprite or bird,
What sweet thoughts are thine:
I have never heard
Praise or love or wine
That panted forth a flood of rapture so divine.

Chorus Hymeneal
Or triumphal chant,
Matched with thine would be all
But an empty vaunt,
A thing wherein we feel there is some hidden want.

What objects are the fountains
Of thy happy strain?
What fields, or waves, or mountains?
What shapes of sky or plain?
What love of thine own kind? what ignorance of pain?

With thy clear keen joyance
Langour cannot be:
Shadow of annoyance
Never came near thee:
Thou lovest – but ne'er knew love's sad satiety.

Waking or asleep,
   Thou of death must deem
Things more true and deep
   Than we mortals dream,
Or how could thy notes flow in such a crystal stream?

We look before and after,
   And pine for what is not:
Our sincerest laughter
   With some pain is fraught;
Our sweetest songs are those that tell of saddest thought.

Yet if we could scorn
   Hate, and pride, and fear;
If we were things born
   Not to shed a tear,
I know not how thy joy we ever should come near.

Better than all measures
   Of delightful sound,
Better than all treasures
   That in books are found,
Thy skill to poet were, thou scorner of the ground!

Teach me half the gladness
   That thy brain must know,
Such harmonious madness
   From my lips would flow,
The world should listen then – as I am listening now.

PERCY BYSSHE SHELLEY (1792–1822)

Mountain Flowers

❧❧❧

TREAD softly!   For I think the gentian
    is blue enamel on the smooth green grass,
painted long since by some Italian
    or Dutch artificer in coloured glass;
and still more softly when you reach the Pass!
    For, though these are narcissus, the same man
used them for tapers, lighting at High Mass
    the blue-green windows of a Vatican.
Take off your shoes!   Tread very soft and slowly!
    For, though we can no longer walk beside him,
    the mountain-path is still the way love goes,
and, where his feet have been, the ground is holy,
    and those small bushes, though all else denied him,
    burn with the torches of his Alpine rose.

HUMBERT WOLFE (1885–1940)

The Daffodils

I WANDERED lonely as a cloud
   That floats on high o'er vales and hills,
When all at once I saw a crowd,
   A host, of golden daffodils;
Beside the lake, beneath the trees,
Fluttering and dancing in the breeze.

Continuous as the stars that shine
   And twinkle on the Milky Way,
They stretched in never-ending line
   Along the margin of a bay:
Ten thousand saw I at a glance,
Tossing their heads in sprightly dance.

The waves beside them danced; but they
   Out-did the sparkling waves in glee:
A poet could not but be gay,
   In such a jocund company:
I gazed – and gazed – but little thought
What wealth the show to me had brought:

For oft, when on my couch I lie
   In vacant or in pensive mood,
They flash upon that inward eye
   Which is the bliss of solitude;
And then my heart with pleasure fills,
And dances with the daffodils.

WILLIAM WORDSWORTH (1770–1850)

THE SEASONS

August

From: *The Shepherd's Calendar*

HARVEST approaches with its busy day
The wheat tans brown and barley bleaches grey
In yellow garb the oatland intervenes
And tawney glooms the valley thronged with beans
Silent the village grows, wood wandering dreams
Seem not so lovely as its quiet seems
Doors are shut up as on a winters day
And not a child about them lies at play
The dust that winnows neath the breezes feet
Is all that stirs about the silent street
Fancy might think that deserts spreading fear
Had whispered terror into quiets ear
Or plundering armies past the place had come
And drove the lost inhabitants from home
The fields now claim them where a motley crew
Of old and young their daily tasks pursue
The barleys beard is grey and wheat is brown
And wakens toil betimes to leave the town
The reapers leave their beds before the sun
And gleaners follow when home toils are done
To pick the littered ear the reaper leaves
And glean in open fields among the sheaves.

The fields are all alive with busy noise
Of labours sounds and insects humming joys
Some oer the glittering sickle sweating stoop
Startling full oft the partridge coveys up
Some oer the rustling scythe go bending on
And shockers follow where their toils have gone
First turning swaths to wither in the sun
Where mice from terrors dangers nimbly run
Leaving their tender young in fears alarm
Lapt up in nests of chimbled grasses warm
And oft themselves for safety search in vain
From the rude boy or churlish hearted swain

Who beat their stone chinkd forks about the ground
And spread an instant murder all around
Tho oft the anxious maidens tender prayer
Urges the clown their little lives to spare
Who sighs while trailing the long rake along
At scenes so cruel and forgets her song
And stays wi love his murder aiming hand
Some ted the puffing winnow down the land
And others following roll them up in heaps
While cleanly as a barn door beesome sweeps
The hawling drag wi gathering weeds entwind
And singing rakers end the toils behind.

JOHN CLARE (1793–1864)

September

Now every day the bracken browner grows,
    Even the purple stars
    Of clematis, that shone about the bars,
Grow browner; and the little autumn rose
    Dons, for her rosy gown,
    Sad weeds of brown.

Now falls the eve; and ere the morning sun,
    Many a flower her sweet life will have lost,
    Slain by the bitter frost,
Who slays the butterflies also, one by one,
    The tiny beasts
    That go about their business and their feasts.

MARY COLERIDGE (1861–1907)

Song at the Beginning of Autumn

Now watch this autumn that arrives
In smells. All looks like summer still;
Colours are quite unchanged, the air
On green and white serenely thrives.
Heavy the trees with growth and full
The fields. Flowers flourish everywhere.

Proust who collected time within
A child's cake would understand
The ambiguity of this –
Summer still raging while a thin
Column of smoke stirs from the land
Proving that autumn gropes for us.

But every season is a kind
Of rich nostalgia. We give names –
Autumn and summer, winter, spring –
As though to unfasten from the mind
Our moods and give them outward forms.
We want the certain, solid thing.
But I am carried back against
My will into a childhood where
Autumn is bonfires, marbles, smoke;
I lean against my window fenced
From evocations in the air.
When I said autumn, autumn broke.

ELIZABETH JENNINGS (1926–   )

To Autumn

Season of mists and mellow fruitfulness,
    Close bosom-friend of the maturing sun;
Conspiring with him how to load and bless
    With fruit the vines that round the thatch-eaves run;
To bend with apples the moss'd cottage-trees,
    And fill all fruit with ripeness to the core;
        To swell the gourd, and plump the hazel shells
With a sweet kernel; to set budding more,
And still more, later flowers for the bees,
Until they think warm days will never cease,
        For Summer has o'er-brimm'd their clammy cells.

Who hath not seen thee oft amid thy store?
    Sometimes whoever seeks abroad may find
Thee sitting careless on a granary floor,
    Thy hair soft-lifted by the winnowing wind;
Or on a half-reap'd furrow sound asleep,
    Drows'd with the fume of poppies, while thy hook
        Spares the next swath and all its twinèd flowers;
And sometimes like a gleaner thou dost keep
    Steady thy laden head across a brook;
    Or by a cider-press, with patient look,
        Thou watchest the last oozings, hours by hours.

Where are the songs of Spring? Ay, where are they?
    Think not of them, thou hast thy music too, —
While barrèd clouds bloom the soft-dying day,
    And touch the stubble-plains with rosy hue;
Then in a wailful choir the small gnats mourn
    Among the river sallows, borne aloft
        Or sinking as the light wind lives or dies;
And full-grown lambs loud bleat from hilly bourn;
    Hedge-crickets sing; and now with treble soft
    The redbreast whistles from a garden-croft;
        And gathering swallows twitter in the skies.

JOHN KEATS (1795–1821)

Thomas Gainsborough (1727–1788) *The Woodcutter's House*, Belvoir Castle, Rutland

George Morland (1763–1804) *A Man Smoking a Pipe by an Inn Fire*, Private Collection

April Rise

If EVER I saw blessing in the air
    I see it now in this still early day
Where lemon-green the vaporous morning drips
    Wet sunlight on the powder of my eye.

Blown bubble-film of blue, the sky wraps round
    Weeds of warm light whose every root and rod
Splutters with soapy green, and all the world
    Sweats with the bead of summer in its bud.

If ever I heard blessing it is there
    Where birds in trees that shoals and shadows are
Splash with their hidden wings and drops of sound
    Break on my ears their crests of throbbing air.

Pure in the haze the emerald sun dilates,
    The lips of sparrows milk the mossy stones,
While white as water by the lake a girl
    Swims her green hand among the gathered swans.

Now, as the almond burns its smoking wick,
    Dropping small flames to light the candled grass;
Now, as my low blood scales its second chance,
    If ever world were blessed, now it is.

LAURIE LEE (1914–)

The West Wind

It's a warm wind, the west wind, full of birds' cries;
I never hear the west wind but tears are in my eyes.
For it comes from the west lands, the old brown hills,
And April's in the west wind, and daffodils.

It's a fine land, the west land, for hearts as tired as mine,
Apple orchards blossom there, and the air's like wine.
There is cool green grass there, where men may lie at rest,
And the thrushes are in song there, fluting from the nest.

'Will ye not come home, brother? Ye have been long away,
It's April, and blossom time, and white is the may;
And bright is the sun, brother, and warm is the rain, –
Will ye not come home, brother, home to us again?

'The young corn is green, brother, where the rabbits run,
It's blue sky, and white clouds, and warm rain and sun.
It's song to a man's soul, brother, fire to a man's brain,
To hear the wild bees and see the merry spring again.

'Larks are singing in the west, brother, above the green wheat,
So will ye not come home, brother, and rest your tired feet?
I've a balm for bruised hearts, brother, sleep for aching eyes,'
Says the warm wind, the west wind, full of birds' cries.

It's the white road westwards is the road I must tread
To the green grass, the cool grass, and rest for heart and head,
To the violets and the warm hearts and the thrushes' song,
In the fine land, the west land, the land where I belong.

JOHN MASEFIELD (1878–1967)

In Early Spring

O SPRING, I know thee!   Seek for sweet surprise
   In the young children's eyes.
But I have learnt the years, and know the yet
   Leaf-folded violet.
Mine ear, awake to silence, can foretell
   The cuckoo's fitful bell.
I wander in a grey time that encloses
   June and the wild hedge-roses.
A year's procession of the flowers doth pass
   My feet, along the grass.
And all you wild birds silent yet, I know
   The notes that stir you so,
Your songs yet half devised in the dim dear
   Beginnings of the year.
In these young days you meditate your part;
   I have it all by heart.

I know the secrets of the seeds of flowers
   Hidden and warm with showers,
And how, in kindling Spring, the cuckoo shall
   Alter his interval.
But not a flower or song I ponder is
   My own, but memory's.
I shall be silent in those days desired
   Before a world inspired.
O all brown birds, compose your old song-phrases
   Earth, thy familiar daisies!

A poet mused upon the dusky height,
    Between two stars towards night,
His purpose in his heart.   I watched, a space,
    The meaning of his face:
There was the secret, fled from earth and skies,
    Hid in his grey young eyes.
My heart and all the Summer wait his choice,
    And wonder for his voice.
Who shall foretell his songs, and who aspire
    But to divine his lyre?
Sweet earth, we know thy dimmest mysteries,
    But he is lord of his.

ALICE MEYNELL (1847–1922)

The Rainy Summer

THERE'S much afoot in heaven and earth this year;
    The winds hunt up the sun, hunt up the moon,
Trouble the dubious dawn, hasten the drear
    Height of a threatening noon.

No breath of boughs, no breath of leaves, of fronds,
    May linger or grow warm; the trees are loud;
The forest, rooted, tosses in her bonds,
    And strains against the cloud.

No scents may pause within the garden-fold;
    The rifled flowers are cold as ocean-shells;
Bees, humming in the storm, carry their cold
    Wild honey to cold cells.

ALICE MEYNELL (1847–1922)

The Leaf Burners

UNDER two oak trees
  on top of the fell,
With an old hawthorn hedge
  to hold off the wind,
I saw the leaf burners
  brushing the leaves
With their long brooms
  into the blaze.
Above them the sky
  scurried along
Pale as a plate,
  and peered thro' the oaks,
While the hurrying wind
  harried the hedge.
But fast as they swept
  feeding the leaves
Into the flame
  that flickered and fumed,

The wind, the tree-shaker,
  shaking the boughs,
Whirled others down
  withered and wan –
Summer's small folk,
  faded and fain
To give up their life;
  earth unto earth,
Ashes to ashes,
  life unto death.

Far on the fell
  where the road ran,
I heard the men march,
  in the mouth of the wind:
And the leaf burners heard
  and leaned down their heads,
Brow upon broom

and let the leaves lie,
And counted their kin
　　that crossed over sea,
And left wife and wean
　　to fight in the war.

Forth over fell
　　I fared on my way;
Yet often looked back,
　　when the wind blew,
To see the flames coil
　　like a curl of bright hair
Round the face of a child –
　　a flower of fire,
Beneath the long boughs
　　where lush and alive,
The leaves flourished long,
　　loving the sun.

Much I thought then
　　of men that went forth,
Or dropt like the leaves,
　　to die and to live;
While the leaf burners
　　with their long brooms
Drew them together
　　on the day of their death.
I wondered at that,
　　walking the fell –
Feeling the wind
　　that wafted the leaves
And set their souls
　　free of the smoke,
Free of the dead,
　　speeding the flame
To spire on the air –
　　a spark that should spring
In me, man of men;
　　last of the leaves.

ERNEST RHYS (1859–1946)

Winter Rain

EVERY valley drinks
Every dell and hollow,
Where the kind rain sinks and sinks,
Green of Spring will follow.

Yet a lapse of weeks —
Buds will burst their edges,
Strip their wool-coats, glue-coats, streaks,
In the woods and hedges;

Weave a bower of love
For birds to meet each other,
Weave a canopy above
Nest and egg and mother.

But for fattening rain
We should have no flowers,
Never a bud or leaf again
But for soaking showers.

CHRISTINA ROSSETTI (1830–1894)

Winter

From: *Love's Labour's Lost*

❦❧

WHEN icicles hang by the wall,
    And Dick the shepherd blows his nail,
And Tom bears logs into the hall,
    And milk comes frozen home in pail,
When blood is nipp'd, and ways be foul,
Then nightly sings the staring owl,
                            Tu-who;
Tu-whit, tu-who – a merry note,
While greasy Joan doth keel the pot.

When all aloud the wind doth blow,
    And coughing drowns the parson's saw,
And birds sit brooding in the snow,
    And Marian's nose looks red and raw,
When roasted crabs hiss in the bowl,
Then nightly sings the staring owl,
                            Tu-who;
Tu-whit, tu-who – a merry note,
While greasy Joan doth keel the pot.

WILLIAM SHAKESPEARE (1564–1616)

Summer and Winter

It was a bright and cheerful afternoon,
Towards the end of the sunny month of June,
When the north wind congregates in crowds
The floating mountains of the silver clouds
From the horizon – and the stainless sky
Opens beyond them like eternity.
All things rejoiced beneath the sun; the weeds,
The river, and the corn-fields, and the reeds;
The willow leaves that glanced in the light breeze,
And the firm foliage of the larger trees.

It was a winter such as when birds die
In the deep forests; and the fishes lie
Stiffened in the translucent ice, which makes
Even the mud and slime of the warm lakes
A wrinkled clod as hard as brick; and when,
Among their children, comfortable men
Gather about great fires, and yet feel cold:
Alas, then, for the homeless beggar old!

PERCY BYSSHE SHELLEY (1792–1822)

NOSTALGIC
AND
REFLECTIVE

A Night Song

Oh! do you wake, or do you sleep
   With window to the full-moon'd sky?
Oh! have you lost, or do you keep
   A thought of all the day gone by?
Or are you dead to all you knew
Of life, the while I live to you?

May air, o'er wallside roses brought,
   Of charming gardens give you dreams;
May rustling leaves beguile your thought
   With dreams of walks by falling streams.
And on your lids be light that yields
Bright dream-clouds over daisied fields.

Our meeting hour of yesterday
   To me, now deep in waning night,
Seems all a glory pass'd away
   Beyond a year – time's longsome flight.
Though night seems far too short to weigh
Your words and deeds of yesterday.

While rise or sink the glittering stars
   Above dim woods, or hillock brows,
There, out within the moonpaled bars,
   In darksome bunches sleep your cows.
So sweetly sleep, asleep be they
Until you meet the opening day.

WILLIAM BARNES (1801–1886)

Forefathers

HERE they went with smock and crook,
   Toiled in the sun, lolled in the shade,
Here they mudded out the brook
   And here their hatchet cleared the glade:
Harvest-supper woke their wit,
Huntsman's moon their wooings lit.

From this church they led their brides,
   From this church themselves were led
Shoulder-high; on these waysides
   Sat to take their beer and bread.
Names are gone – what men they were
These their cottages declare.

Names are vanished, save the few
   In the old brown Bible scrawled;
These were men of pith and thew,
   Whom the city never called;
Scarce could read or hold a quill,
Built the barn, the forge, the mill.

On the green they watched their sons
   Playing till too dark to see,
As their fathers watched them once,
   As my father once watched me;
While the bat and beetle flew
On the warm air webbed with dew.

Unrecorded, unrenowned,
    Men from whom my ways begin,
Here I know you by your ground
    But I know you not within –
There is silence, there survives
Not a moment of your lives.

Like the bee that now is blown
    Honey-heavy on my hand,
From his toppling tansy-throne
    In the green tempestuous land –
I'm in clover now, nor know
Who made honey long ago.

EDMUND BLUNDEN (1896–1974)

These I Have Loved

WHITE plates and cups, clean-gleaming,
Ringed with blue lines; and feathery, faery dust;
Wet roofs, beneath the lamp-light; the strong crust
Of friendly bread; and many-tasting food;
Rainbows; and the blue bitter smoke of wood;
And radiant raindrops couching in cool flowers;
And flowers themselves, that sway through sunny hours,
Dreaming of moths that drink them under the moon;
Then, the cool kindliness of sheets, that soon
Smooth away trouble; and the rough male kiss
Of blankets; grainy wood; live hair that is
Shining and free; blue-massing clouds; the keen
Unpassioned beauty of a great machine;
The benison of hot water; furs to touch;
The good smell of old clothes; and other such –
The comfortable smell of friendly fingers,
Hair's fragrance, and the musty reek that lingers
About dead leaves and last year's ferns . . .
                                    Dear names,
And thousand other throng to me! Royal flames;
Sweet water's dimpling laugh from tap or spring;
Holes in the ground; and voices that do sing;
Voices in laughter, too; and body's pain,
Soon turned to peace; and the deep-panting train;
Firm sands; the little dulling edge of foam
That browns and dwindles as the wave goes home . . .
All these have been my loves . . .

RUPERT BROOKE (1887–1915)

Home-Thoughts, from Abroad

OH, to be in England
Now that April's there,
And whoever wakes in England
Sees, some morning, unaware,
That the lowest boughs and the brushwood sheaf
Round the elm-tree bole are in tiny leaf,
While the chaffinch sings on the orchard bough
In England – now!

And after April, when May follows,
And the whitethroat builds, and all the swallows –
Hark! where my blossomed pear-tree in the hedge
Leans to the field and scatters on the clover
Blossoms and dewdrops – at the bent spray's edge –
That's the wise thrush; he sings each song twice over,
Lest you should think he never could recapture
The first fine careless rapture!
And though the fields look rough with hoary dew,
All will be gay when noontide wakes anew
The buttercups, the little children's dower
– Far brighter than this gaudy melon-flower!

ROBERT BROWNING (1812–1889)

An Old Woman of the Roads

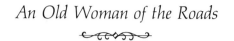

O, TO have a little house!
To own the hearth and stool and all!
The heaped up sods upon the fire,
The pile of turf against the wall!

To have a clock with weights and chains
And pendulum swinging up and down!
A dresser filled with shining delph,
Speckled and white and blue and brown!

I could be busy all the day
Clearing and sweeping hearth and floor,
And fixing on their shelf again
My white and blue and speckled store!

I could be quiet there at night
Beside the fire and by myself,
Sure of a bed, and loth to leave
The ticking clock and the shining delph!

Och! but I'm weary of mist and dark,
And roads where there's never a house nor bush,
And tired I am of bog and road
And the crying wind and the lonesome hush!

And I am praying to God on high,
And I am praying Him night and day,
For a little house – a house of my own –
Out of the wind's and the rain's way.

PADRAIC COLUM (1881–1972)

Jean-Honoré Fragonard (1732–1806) *The Swing*, The Wallace Collection, London

James Archer (1823–1904) *Robert Burns and Highland Mary*, Roy Miles Fine Paintings, London

Anacreontics

I Drinking

THE thirsty earth soaks up the rain,
And drinks and gapes for drink again;
The plants suck in the earth, and are
With constant drinking fresh and fair;
The sea itself (which one would think
Should have but little need of drink)
Drinks twice ten thousand rivers up,
So fill'd that they o'erflow the cup.
The busy Sun (and one would guess
By 's drunken fiery face no less)
Drinks up the sea, and when he's done,
The Moon and Stars drink up the Sun:
They drink and dance by their own light,
They drink and revel all the night:
Nothing in Nature's sober found,
But an eternal health goes round.
Fill up the bowl, then, fill it high,
Fill all the glasses there – for why
Should every creature drink but I?
Why, man of morals, tell me why?

ABRAHAM COWLEY (1618–1667)

Leisure

WHAT is this life if, full of care,
We have no time to stand and stare?

No time to stand beneath the boughs
And stare as long as sheep or cows.

No time to see, when woods we pass,
Where squirrels hide their nuts in grass.

No time to see, in broad daylight,
Streams full of stars like skies at night.

No time to turn at Beauty's glance,
And watch her feet, how they can dance.

No time to wait till her mouth can
Enrich that smile her eyes began.

A poor life this if, full of care,
We have no time to stand and stare.

W. H. DAVIES (1871–1940)

All That's Past

Very old are the woods;
    And the buds that break
Out of the brier's boughs,
    When March winds wake,
So old with their beauty are –
    Oh, no man knows
Through what wild centuries
    Roves back the rose.

Very old are the brooks;
    And the rills that rise
Where snow sleeps cold beneath
    The azure skies
Sing such a history
    Of come and gone,
Their every drop is as wise
    As Solomon.

Very old are we men;
    Our dreams are tales
Told in dim Eden
    By Eve's nightingales;
We wake and whisper awhile,
    But, the day gone by,
Silence and sleep like fields
    Of amaranth lie.

WALTER DE LA MARE (1873–1956)

The Midlands

Black in the summer night my Cotswold hill
　　Aslant my window sleeps, beneath a sky
Deep as the bedded violets that fill
　　March woods with dusky passion. As I lie
Abed between cool walls I watch the host
　　Of the slow stars lit over Gloucester plain,
And drowsily the habit of these most
　　Beloved English lands moves in my brain,
While silence holds dominion of the dark,
Save when the foxes from the spinneys bark.

I see the valleys in their morning mist
　　Wreathed under limpid hills in moving light,
Happy with many a yeoman melodist;
　　I see the little roads of twinkling white
Busy with fieldward teams and market gear
　　Of rosy men, cloth-gaitered, who can tell
The many-minded changes of the year,
　　Who knows why crops and kine fare ill or well;
I see the sun persuade the mist away,
Till town and stead are shining to the day.

I see the wagons move along the rows
　　Of ripe and summer-breathing clover-flower,
I see the lissom husbandman who knows
　　Deep in his heart the beauty of his power,
As lithely pitched, the full-heaped fork bids on
　　The harvest home. I hear the rickyard fill
With gossip as in generations gone,
　　While wagon follows wagon from the hill.
I think how, when our seasons all are sealed,
Shall come the unchanging harvest from the field.

I see the barns and comely manors planned
    By men who somehow moved in comely thought,
Who, with a simple shippon to their hand,
    As men upon some godlike business wrought;
I see the little cottages that keep
    Their beauty still where since Plantagenet
Have come the shepherds happily to sleep,
    Finding the loaves and cups of cider set;
I see the twisted shepherds, brown and old,
Driving at dusk their glimmering sheep to fold.

And now the valleys that upon the sun
    Broke from their opal veils, are veil'd again,
And the last light upon the wolds is done,
    And silence falls on flock and fields and men;
And black upon the night I watch my hill,
    And the stars shine, and there an owly wing
Brushes the night, and all again is still,
    And, from this land of worship that I sing,
I turn to sleep, content that from my sires
I draw the blood of England's midmost shires.

JOHN DRINKWATER (1882–1937)

Afterwards

WHEN the Present has latched its postern behind my tremulous
      stay,
   And the May month flaps its glad green leaves like wings,
Delicate-filmed as new-spun silk, will the neighbours say,
   'He was a man who used to notice such things'?

If it be in the dusk when, like an eyelid's soundless blink,
   The dewfall-hawk comes crossing the shades to alight
Upon the wind-warped upland thorn, a gazer may think,
   'To him this must have been a familiar sight.'

If I pass during some nocturnal blackness, mothy and warm,
   When the hedgehog travels furtively over the lawn,
One may say, 'He strove that such innocent creatures should
      come to no harm,
   But he could do little for them; and now he is gone.'

If, when hearing that I have been stilled at last, they stand at
      the door,
   Watching the full-starred heavens that winter sees,
Will this thought rise on those who will meet my face no more,
   'He was one who had an eye for such mysteries'?

And will any say when my bell of quittance is heard in the
      gloom,
   And a crossing breeze cuts a pause in its outrollings,
Till they rise again, as they were a new bell's boom,
   'He hears it not now, but used to notice such things'?

THOMAS HARDY (1840–1928)

Great Things

SWEET cyder is a great thing,
   A great thing to me,
Spinning down to Weymouth town
   By Ridgway thirstily,
And maid and mistress summoning
   Who tend the hostelry:
O cyder is a great thing,
   A great thing to me!

The dance it is a great thing,
   A great thing to me,
With candles lit and partners fit
   For night-long revelry;
And going home when day-dawning
   Peeps pale upon the lea:
O dancing is a great thing,
   A great thing to me!

Love is, yea, a great thing,
   A great thing to me,
When, having drawn across the lawn
   In darkness silently,
A figure flits like one a-wing
   Out from the nearest tree:
O love is, yes, a great thing,
   A great thing to me!

THOMAS HARDY (1840–1928)

A Shropshire Lad

XXXI

On Wenlock Edge the wood's in trouble;
　　His forest fleece the Wrekin heaves;
The gale, it plies the saplings double,
　　And thick on Severn snow the leaves.

'Twould blow like this through holt and hanger
　　When Uricon the city stood:
'Tis the old wind in the old anger,
　　But then it threshed another wood.

Then, 'twas before my time, the Roman
　　At yonder heaving hill would stare:
The blood that warms an English yeoman,
　　The thoughts that hurt him, they were there.

There, like the wind through woods in riot,
　　Through him the gale of life blew high;
The tree of man was never quiet:
　　Then 'twas the Roman, now 'tis I.

The gale, it plies the saplings double,
　　It blows so hard, 'twill soon be gone:
To-day the Roman and his trouble
　　Are ashes under Uricon.

A. E. HOUSMAN (1859–1936)

From: *Endymion*

LEADING the way, young damsels danced along,
Bearing the burden of a shepherd song;
Each having a white wicker over brimm'd
With April's tender younglings: next, well trimm'd,
A crowd of shepherds with as sunburnt looks
As may be read of in Arcadian books;
Such as sat listening round Apollo's pipe,
When the great deity, for earth too ripe,
Let his divinity o'erflowing die
In music, through the vales of Thessaly;
Some idly trail'd their sheep-hooks on the ground,
And some kept up a shrilly mellow sound
With ebon-tipped flutes; close after these,
Now coming from beneath the forest trees,
A venerable priest full soberly,
Begirt with minist'ring looks: always his eye
Stedfast upon the matted turf he kept,
And after him his sacred vestments swept.

From his right hand there swung a vase, milk-white,
Of mingled wine, out-sparkling generous light:
And in his left he held a basket full
Of all sweet herbs that searching eye could cull:
Wild thyme, and valley-lillies whiter still
Than Leda's love, and cresses from the rill.
His aged head, crowned with beechen wreath,
Seem'd like a poll of ivy in the teeth
Of winter hoar. Then came another crowd
Of shepherds, lifting in due time aloud
Their share of the ditty. After them appear'd,
Up-followed by a multitude that rear'd
Their voices to the clouds, a fair wrought car,
Easily rolling so as scarce to mar
The freedom of three steeds of dapple brown:
Who stood therein did seem of great renown
Among the throng. His youth was fully blown,
Showing like Ganymede to manhood grown;

And, for those simple times, his garments were
A chieftain king's: beneath his breast, half bare,
Was hung a silver bugle, and between
His nervy knees there lay a boar-spear keen.
A smile was on his countenance; he seem'd,
To common lookers on, like one who dream'd
Of idleness in groves Elysian:
But there were some who feelingly could scan
A lurking trouble in his nether lip,
And see that oftentimes the reins would slip
Through his forgotten hands: then would they sigh,
And think of yellow leaves, of owlets' cry,
Of logs piled solemnly. – Ah, well-a-day,
Why should our young Endymion pine away?

JOHN KEATS (1795–1821)

The Way Through
the Woods

THEY SHUT the road through the woods
Seventy years ago.
Weather and rain have undone it again,
And now you would never know
There was once a road through the woods
Before they planted the trees.
It is underneath the coppice and heath,
And the thin anemones.
Only the keeper sees
That, where the ring-dove broods,
And the badgers roll at ease,
There was once a road through the woods.

Yet, if you enter the woods
Of a summer evening late,
When the night-air cools on the trout-ringed pools
Where the otter whistles his mate,
(They fear not men in the woods,
Because they see so few.)
You will hear the beat of a horse's feet
And the swish of a skirt in the dew,
Steadily cantering through
The misty solitudes,
As though they perfectly knew
The old lost road through the woods.
But there is no road through the woods.

RUDYARD KIPLING (1865–1936)

Ode on Solitude

HAPPY the man, whose wish and care
    A few paternal acres bound,
Content to breathe his native air,
       In his own ground.

Whose herds with milk, whose fields with bread,
    Whose flocks supply him with attire,
Whose trees in summer yield him shade,
       In winter fire.

Blest, who can unconcern'dly find
    Hours, days, and years slide soft away,
In health of body, peace of mind,
       Quiet by day,

Sound sleep by night; study and ease,
    Together mixt; sweet recreation,
And innocence, which most does please
       With meditation.

Thus let me live, unseen, unknown;
    Thus unlamented let me die;
Steal from the world, and not a stone
       Tell where I lie.

ALEXANDER POPE (1688–1744)

RURAL LOVE

The Rosebud

QUEEN of fragrance, lovely Rose,
The beauties of thy leaves disclose!
– But thou, fair Nymph, thyself survey
In this sweet offspring of a day.
That miracle of face must fail,
Thy charms are sweet, but charms are frail:
Swift as the short-lived flower they fly,
At morn they bloom, at evening die:
Though Sickness yet a while forbears,
Yet Time destroys what Sickness spares:
Now Helen lives alone in fame,
And Cleopatra's but a name:
Time must indent that heavenly brow,
And thou must be what they are now.

WILLIAM BROOME (1689–1745)

Truly Great

My walls outside must have some flowers,
  My walls within must have some books;
A house that's small; a garden large,
  And in it leafy nooks.

A little gold that's sure each week;
  That comes not from my living kind,
But from a dead man in his grave,
  Who cannot change his mind:

A lovely wife, and gentle too;
  Contented that no eyes but mine
Can see her many charms, nor voice
  To call her beauty fine:

Where she would in that stone cage live,
  A self-made prisoner with me;
While many a wild bird sang around,
  On gate, on bush, on tree.

And she sometimes to answer them,
  In her far sweeter voice than all;
Till birds, that loved to look on leaves,
  Will doat on a stone wall.

With this small house, this garden large,
  This little gold, this lovely mate,
With health in body, peace at heart —
  Show me a man more great.

W. H. DAVIES (1871–1940)

The Passionate Shepherd to his Love

Come live with me and be my Love,
And we will the pleasures prove
That hills and valleys, dale and field,
And all the craggy mountains yield.

There will we sit upon the rocks
And see the shepherds feed their flocks,
By shallow rivers, to whose falls
Melodious birds sing madrigals.

There will I make thee beds of roses
And a thousand fragrant posies,
A cap of flowers, and a kirtle
Embroider'd all with leaves of myrtle.

A gown made of the finest wool,
Which from our pretty lambs we pull,
Fair linèd slippers for the cold,
With buckles of the purest gold.

A belt of straw and ivy buds
With coral clasps and amber studs:
And if these pleasures may thee move,
Come live with me and be my Love.

The shepherd swains shall dance and sing
For thy delight each May-morning:
If these delights thy mind may move,
Then live with me and be my Love.

CHRISTOPHER MARLOWE (1564–1593)

Jean Baptiste Guillaumin (1841–1927) *Madame Guillaumin Fishing*, Connaught Brown, London

Sir George Clausen (1852–1944) *The Mowers*, Usher Gallery, Lincoln

Song

I MADE another garden, yea,
    For my new Love:
I left the dead rose where it lay
    And set the new above.
Why did my summer not begin?
    Why did my heart not haste?
My old Love came and walked therein,
    And laid the garden waste.

She entered with her weary smile,
    Just as of old;
She looked around a little while
    And shivered at the cold:
Her passing touch was death to all,
    Her passing look a blight;
She made the white-rose petals fall,
    And turn'd the red rose white.

Her pale robe clinging to the grass
    Seemed like a snake
That bit the grass and ground, alas!
    And a sad trail did make.
She went up slowly to the gate,
    And then, just as of yore,
She turn'd back at the last to wait
    And say farewell once more.

ARTHUR O'SHAUGHNESSY (1844–1881)

The Nymph's Reply to the Shepherd

If ALL the world and love were young,
And truth in every shepherd's tongue,
These pretty pleasures might me move
To live with thee and be thy Love.

But Time drives flocks from field to fold;
When rivers rage and rocks grow cold;
And Philomel becometh dumb;
The rest complains of cares to come.

The flowers do fade, and wanton fields
To wayward Winter reckoning yields:
A honey tongue, a heart of gall,
Is fancy's spring, but sorrow's fall.

Thy gowns, thy shoes, thy beds of roses,
Thy cap, thy kirtle, and thy posies,
Soon break, soon wither – soon forgotten,
In folly ripe, in reason rotten.

Thy belt of straw and ivy-buds,
Thy coral clasps and amber studs,
All these in me no means can move
To come to thee and be thy Love.

But could youth last, and love still breed,
Had joys no date, nor age no need,
Then these delights my mind might move
To live with thee and be thy Love.

SIR WALTER RALEGH (1552?–1618)

The Kiss

Coming to kiss her lips (such grace I found)
　　Meseemed I smelt a garden of sweet flowers,
That dainty odours from them threw around
　　For damsels fit to deck their lovers' bowers.
Her lips did smell like unto gillyflowers,
　　Her ruddy cheeks like unto roses red,
Her snowy brows like budded belamours,
　　Her lovely eyes like pinks but newly spread;
Her goodly bosom like a strawberry bed,
　　Her neck like to a bunch of columbines,
Her breast like lilies ere their leaves be shed;
　　Her nipples like young blossomed jessamines.
　　　Such fragrant flowers do give most odorous smell;
　　But her sweet odour did them all excel.

EDMUND SPENSER (1522?–1599)

Daisy

WHERE the thistle lifts a purple crown
    Six foot out of the turf,
And the harebell shakes on the windy hill —
    O the breath of the distant surf! —

The hills look over on the South,
    And southward dreams the sea;
And, with the sea-breeze hand in hand,
    Came innocence and she.

Where 'mid the gorse the raspberry
    Red for the gatherer springs,
Two children did we stray and talk
    Wise, idle, childish things.

She listened with big-lipped surprise,
    Breast-deep 'mid flower and spine:
Her skin was like a grape, whose veins
    Run snow instead of wine.

She knew not those sweet words she spake,
    Nor knew her own sweet way;
But there's never a bird, so sweet a song
    Thronged in whose throat that day!

Oh, there were flowers in Storrington
    On the turf and on the spray;
But the sweetest flower on Sussex hills
    Was the Daisy-flower that day!

Her beauty smoothed earth's furrowed face!
    She gave me tokens three: —
A look, a word of her winsome mouth,
    And a wild raspberry.

A berry red, a guileless look,
    A still word, – strings of sand!
And yet they made my wild, wild heart
    Fly down to her little hand.

For, standing artless as the air,
    And candid as the skies,
She took the berries with her hand,
    And the love with her sweet eyes.

The fairest things have fleetest end:
    Their scent survives their close:
But the rose's scent is bitterness
    To him that loved the rose!

She looked a little wistfully
    Then went her sunshine way: –
The sea's eye had a mist on it,
    And the leaves fell from the day.

She went her unremembering way,
    She went, and left in me
The pang of all the partings gone,
    And partings yet to be.

She left me marvelling why my soul
    Was sad that she was glad;
At all the sadness in the sweet,
    The sweetness in the sad.

Still, still I seemed to see her, still
    Look up with soft replies,
And take the berries with her hand,
    And the love with her lovely eyes.

Nothing begins, and nothing ends,
    That is not paid with moan;
For we are born in other's pain,
    And perish in our own.

FRANCIS THOMPSON (1859–1907)

The Song of Wandering Aengus

I WENT out to the hazel wood,
Because a fire was in my head,
And cut and peeled a hazel wand,
And hooked a berry to a thread;
And when white moths were on the wing,
And moth-like stars were flickering out,
I dropped the berry in a stream
And caught a little silver trout.

When I had laid it on the floor
I went to blow the fire aflame,
But something rustled on the floor,
And someone called me by my name:
It had become a glimmering girl
With apple blossom in her hair
Who called me by my name and ran
And faded through the brightening air.

Though I am old with wandering
Through hollow lands and hilly lands
I will find out where she has gone,
And kiss her lips and take her hands;
And walk among long dappled grass,
And pluck till time and times are done
The silver apples of the moon,
The golden apples of the sun.

W. B. YEATS (1865–1939)

Aengus: the god of Love in Irish mythology.

Prothalamion

WHEN the evening came my love said to me:
  Let us go into the garden now that the sky is cool;
The garden of black hellebore and rosemary,
  Where wild woodruff spills in a milky pool.

Low we passed in the twilight, for the wavering heat
  Of day had waned; and round that shaded plot
Of secret beauty the thickets clustered sweet:
  Here is heaven, our hearts whispered, but our lips spake
    not.

Between that old garden and the seas of lazy foam
  Gloomy and beautiful alleys of trees arise
With spire of cypress and dreamy beechen dome,
  So dark that our enchanted sight knew nothing but the
    skies:

Veiled with a soft air, drench'd in the roses' musk
  Or the dusky, dark carnation's breath of clove:
No stars burned in their deeps, but through the dusk
  I saw my love's eyes, and they were brimmed with love.

No star their secret ravished, no wasting moon
  Mocked the sad transience of those eternal hours:
Only the soft, unseeing heaven of June,
  The ghosts of great trees, and the sleeping flowers.

For doves that crooned in the leafy noonday now
  Were silent; the night-jar sought his secret covers,
Nor even a mild sea-whisper moved a creaking bough –
  Was ever a silence deeper made for lovers?

Was ever a moment meeter made for love?
  Beautiful are your close lips beneath my kiss;
And all your yielding sweetness beautiful –
  Oh, never in all the world was such a night as this!

FRANCIS BRETT YOUNG (1884–1954)

COUNTRY
LIVING

From: *The Cotter's Saturday Night*

Let not ambition mock their useful toil,
    Their homely joys, and destiny obscure;
Nor grandeur hear, with a disdainful smile,
    The short but simple annals of the poor.

GRAY

My loved, my honoured, much respected friend!
No mercenary bard his homage pays;
With honest pride I scorn each selfish end:
My dearest meed, a friend's esteem and praise:
To you I sing, in simple Scottish lays,
The lowly train in life's sequestered scene;
The native feelings strong, the guileless ways;
What Aiken in a cottage would have been;
Ah! though his worth unknown, far happier there, I ween.

November chill blaws loud wi' angry sugh;
The shortening winter-day is near a close;
The miry beasts retreating frae the pleugh;
The blackening trains o' craws to their repose:
The toil-worn Cotter frae his labour goes,
This night his weekly moil is at an end,
Collects his spades, his mattocks, and his hoes,
Hoping the morn in ease and rest to spend.
And weary, o'er the moor his course does hameward bend.

At length his lonely cot appears in view,
Beneath the shelter of an aged tree;
The expectant wee-things, toddlin, stacher through
To meet their Dad, wi' flichterin[1] noise an' glee.   [1] contentious
His wee bit ingle, blinking bonnily,
His clean hearthstane, his thriftie wifie's smile,
The lisping infant prattling on his knee,
Does a' his weary carking cares beguile,
An' makes him quite forget his labour an' his toil.

Belyve[2] the elder bairns come drapping in,   [2] by and by
At service out, amang the farmers roun',
Some ca' the pleugh, some herd, some tentie[3] rin   [3] careful
A cannie errand to a neebor town:
Their eldest hope, their Jenny, woman grown,
In youthfu' bloom, love sparkling in her e'e,
Comes hame, perhaps, to shew a braw new gown,
Or deposite her sair-won penny-fee,
To help her parents dear, if they in hardship be.

Wi' joy unfeigned brothers and sisters meet,
An' each for other's weelfare kindly spiers[4]:   [4] inquires
The social hours, swift-winged, unnoticed fleet;
Each tells the uncos[5] that he sees or hears: [5] news
The parents, partial, eye their hopeful years;
Anticipation forward points the view.
The mother, wi' her needle an' her shears,
Gars[6] auld claes look amaist as weel's the new;   [6] makes
The father mixes a' wi' admonition due.

Their masters' an' their mistresses' command,
The younkers a' are warned to obey,
An' mind their labours wi' an eydent[7] hand,   [7] diligent
An' ne'er, though out o' sight, to jauk or play:
'An' O! be sure to fear the Lord alway!
An' mind your duty duly, morn an' night!
Lest in temptation's path ye gang astray,
Implore His counsel and assisting might:
They never sought in vain that sought the Lord aright!'

But hark! a rap comes gently to the door;
Jenny, wha kens the meaning o' the same,
Tells how a neebor lad cam' o'er the moor,
To do some errands, and convoy her hame.
The wily mother sees the conscious flame —
Sparkle in Jenny's e'e, and flush her cheek;
With heart-struck anxious care, inquires his name,
While Jenny hafilins[8] is afraid to speak: [8] half
Weel pleased the mother hears it's nae wild, worthless rake.

Wi' kindly welcome Jenny brings him ben[9],   [9] into the parlour
    A strappan youth; he taks the mother's eye;
Blithe Jenny sees the visit's no ill ta'en;
The father cracks of horses, pleughs, and kye[10]:   [10] cattle
The youngster's artless heart o'erflows wi' joy.
But blate[11] and laithfu'[12], scarce can weel behave;   [11] bashful
The mother, wi' a woman's wiles, can spy   [12] sheepish
What makes the youth sae bashfu' an' sae grave;
Weel pleased to think her bairn's respected like the lave[13]. [13] rest

O happy love! where love like this is found!
O heartfelt raptures! bliss beyond compare!
I've paced much this weary mortal round,
And sage experience bids me this declare —
'If Heaven a draught of heavenly pleasure spare,
One cordial in this melancholy vale,
'Tis when a youthful, loving, modest pair,
In other's arms breathe out the tender tale,
Beneath the milk-white thorn that scents the evening gale.'

Is there, in human form, that bears a heart —
A wretch! a villain! lost to love and truth!
That can, with studied, sly, ensnaring art,
Betray sweet Jenny's unsuspecting youth?
Curse on his perjured arts! dissembling smooth!
Are honour, virtue, conscience, all exiled?
Is there no pity, no relenting ruth,
Points to the parents fondling o'er their child?
Then paints the ruined maid, and their distraction wild?

But now the supper crowns their simple board,
The halesome parritch, chief o' Scotia's food:
The soupe their only Hawkie[14] does afford,   [14] cow
That 'yont the hallant[15] snugly chows her cood: [15] wall
The dame brings forth in complimental mood,
To grace the lad, her weel-hained kebbuck,[16] fell,   [16] well-saved
An' aft he's prest, an' aft he ca's it guid;   cheese
The frugal wifie, garrulous, will tell,   [17] twelve-month
How 'twas a towmond[17] auld, sin' lint was i' the bell[18].
                                    [18] flax was in blossom

The cheerfu' supper done, wi' serious face,
They round the ingle form a circle wide;
The sire turns o'er, wi' patriarchal grace,
The big ha' Bible, ance his father's pride:
His bonnet rev'rently is laid aside,
His lyart haffets[19] wearing thin an' bare;   [19] grey hair
Those strains that once did sweet in Zion glide,
He wales[20] a portion with judicious care;   [20] chooses
And 'Let us worship God!' he says, with solemn air.

They chant their artless notes in simple guise;
They tune their hearts, by far the noblest aim:
Perhaps 'Dundee's' wild warbling measures rise,
Or plaintive 'Martyrs', worthy of the name:
Or noble 'Elgin' beets the heavenward flame
The sweetest far of Scotia's holy lays:
Compared with these, Italian trills are tame;
The tickled ears no heartfelt raptures raise;
Nae unison hae they with our Creator's praise.

Compared with this, how poor Religion's pride,
In all the pomp of method, and of art,
When men display to congregations wide,
Devotion's every grace, except the heart!
The Power, incensed, the pageant will desert,
The pompous strain, the sacerdotal stole;
But haply, in some cottage far apart,
May hear, well pleased, the language of the soul;
And in his book of life the inmates poor enrol.

Then homeward all take off their several way;
The youngling cottagers retire to rest:
The parent pair their secret homage pay,
And proffer up to Heaven the warm request
That He who stills the raven's clamorous nest,
And decks the lily fair in flowery pride,
Would, in the way his wisdom sees the best,
For them and for their little ones provide;
But chiefly, in their hearts with grace divine preside.

ROBERT BURNS (1759–1796)

The Joys of the Road

Now the joys of the road are chiefly these:
A crimson touch on the hard-wood trees;

A vagrant's morning wide and blue,
In early fall, when the wind walks, too;

A shadowy highway, cool and brown,
Alluring up and enticing down

From rippled water to dappled swamp,
From purple glory to scarlet pomp;

The outward eye, the quiet will,
And the striding heart from hill to hill;

The tempter apple over the fence;
The cobweb bloom on the yellow quince;

The palish asters along the wood, –
A lyric touch of the solitude;

An open hand, an easy shoe,
And a hope to make the day go through, –

Another to sleep with, and a third
To wake me up at the voice of a bird;

A scrap of gossip at the ferry;
A comrade neither glum nor merry,

Who never defers and never demands,
But, smiling, takes the world in his hands, –

Seeing it good as when God first saw
And gave it the weight of His will for law.

And O the joy that is never won,
But follows and follows the journeying sun,

By marsh and tide, by meadow and stream,
A will-o'-the-wind, a light-o'-dream,

The racy smell of the forest loam,
When the stealthy, sad-heart leaves go home;

The broad gold wake of the afternoon;
The silent fleck of the cold new moon;

The sound of the hollow sea's release
From the stormy tumult to starry peace;

With only another league to wend;
And two brown arms at the journey's end!

These are the joys of the open road –
For him who travels without a load.

W. BLISS CARMAN (1861–1929)

Coridon's Song

From: *The Compleat Angler* by Izaak Walton

Oн the sweet contentment
The countryman doth find!
　　Heigh trolollie lollie loe,
　　Heigh trollolie lee.
That quiet contemplation
Possesseth all my mind:
　　Then care away,
　　And wend along with me.

For Courts are full of flattery,
As hath too oft been tried;
　　Heigh trollolie lollie loe, etc.
The city full of wantonness
And both are full of pride:
　　Then care away, etc.

But oh, the honest countryman
Speaks truly from his heart,
　　Heigh trollolie lollie loe, etc.
His pride is in his tillage,
His horses, and his cart:
　　Then care away, etc.

Our cloathing is good sheep-skins,
Grey russet for our wives;
　　Heigh trollolie lollie loe, etc.
'Tis warmth and not gay cloathing
That doth prolong our lives:
　　Then care away, etc.

The ploughman, tho' he labour hard,
　　Yet on the holy-day,
　　Heigh trollolie lollie loe, etc.
No emperor so merrily
Does pass his time away:
　　Then care away, etc.

To recompense our tillage,
The heavens afford us showers;
    Heigh trollolie lollie loe, etc.
And for our sweet refreshments
The earth affords us bowers:
    Then care away, etc.

The cuckow and the nightingale
Full merrily do sing,
    Heigh trollolie lollie loe, etc.
And with their pleasant roundelays
Bid welcome to the spring:
    Then care away, etc.

This is not half the happiness
The countryman enjoys;
    Heigh trollolie lollie loe, etc.
Though others think they have as much,
Yet he that says so lies:
    Then come away,
      Turn countrymen with me.

JO CHALKHILL*

*By some supposed to be a pseudonym for Izaak Walton (1593–1683) himself. See note in Introduction.

Oxford Canal

WHEN you have wearied of the valiant spires of this County Town,

Of its wide, white streets and glistening museums, and black monastic walls,

Of its red motors and lumbering trams, and self-sufficient people,

I will take you walking with me to a place you have not seen –

Half town and half country – the land of the Canal.

It is dearer to me than the antique town: I love it more than the rounded hills:

Straightest, sublimest of rivers is the long Canal.

I have observed great storms and trembled; I have wept for fear of the dark.

But nothing makes me so afraid as the clear water of this idle Canal on a summer's noon.

Do you see the great telephone poles down in the water, how every wire is distinct?

If a body fell into the Canal it would rest entangled in those wires for ever, between earth and air.

For the water is as deep as the stars are high.

One day I was thinking how if a man fell from that lofty pole

He would rush through the water toward me till his image was scattered by his splash,

When suddenly a train rushed by: the brazen dome of the engine flashed: the long white carriages roared;

The sun veiled himself for a moment, and the signals loomed in fog;

A savage woman screamed at me from a barge: little children began to cry;

The untidy landscape rose to life; a sawmill started;

A cart rattled down to the wharf, and workmen clanged over the iron footbridge;

A beautiful old man nodded from the first storey window of a square red house,

And a pretty girl came out to hang up clothes in a small
delightful garden.
O strange motion in the suburb of a County Town: slow
regular movements of the dance of death!
Men and not phantoms are these that move in light.
Forgotten they live, and forgotten die.

JAMES ELROY FLECKER (1884–1915)

His Content in the Country

HERE, here I live with what my Board,
Can with the smallest cost afford.
Though ne'r so mean the Viands be,
They well content my *Prew* and me.
Or Pea, or Bean, or Wort, or Beet,
What ever comes, content makes sweet:
Here we rejoyce, because no Rent
We pay for our poore Tenement:
Wherein we rest, and never feare
The Landlord, or the Usurer.
The Quarter-day do's ne'r affright
Our Peacefull slumbers in the night.
We eate our own, and batten more,
Because we feed on no mans score:
But pitie those, whose flanks grow great,
Swel'd with the Lard of others meat.
We blesse our Fortunes, when we see
Our own beloved privacie:
And like our living, where w'are known
To very few, or else to none.

ROBERT HERRICK (1591–1674)

Sussex

GOD gave all men all earth to love,
　　But since our hearts are small,
Ordained for each one spot should prove
　　Beloved over all;
That as He watched Creation's birth,
　　So we, in godlike mood,
May of our love create our earth
　　And see that it is good.

So one shall Baltic pines content,
　　As one some Surrey glade,
Or one the palm-grove's droned lament
　　Before Levuka's trade.
Each to his choice, and I rejoice
　　The lot has fallen to me
In a fair ground – in a fair ground –
　　Yea, Sussex by the sea!

No tender-hearted garden crowns,
　　No bosomed woods adorn
Our blunt, bow-headed, whale-backed Downs,
　　But gnarled and writhen thorn –
Bare slopes where chasing shadows skim,
　　And through the gaps revealed
Belt upon belt, the wooded, dim
　　Blue goodness of the Weald.

Clean of officious fence or hedge,
　　Half-wild and wholly tame,
The wise turf cloaks the white cliff edge
　　As when the Romans came.
What sign of those that fought and died
　　At shift of sword and sword?
The barrow and the camp abide,
　　The sunlight and the sward.

Here leaps ashore the full Sou'west
    All heavy-winged with brine,
Here lies above the folded crest
    The Channel's leaden line;
And here the sea-fogs lap and cling,
    And here, each warning each,
The sheep-bells and the ship-bells ring
    Along the hidden beach.

We have no waters to delight
    Our broad and brookless vales —
Only the dewpond on the height
    Unfed, that never fails,
Whereby no tattered herbage tells
    Which way the season flies —
Only our close-bit thyme that smells
    Like dawn in Paradise.

Here through the strong unhampered days
    The tinkling silence thrills;
Or little, lost, Down churches praise
    The Lord who made the hills:
But here the Old Gods guard their round,
    And, in her secret heart,
The heathen kingdom Wilfred found
    Dreams, as she dwells, apart.

Though all the rest were all my share,
    With equal soul I'd see
Her nine-and-thirty sisters fair,
    Yet none more fair than she.
Choose ye your need from Thames to Tweed,
    And I will choose instead
Such lands as lie 'twixt Rake and Rye
    Black Down and Beachy Head.

I will go out against the sun
    Where the rolled scarp retires,
And the Long Man of Wilmington
    Looks naked toward the shires;
And east till doubting Rother crawls
    To find the fickle tide,
By dry and sea-forgotten walls,
    Our ports of stranded pride.

I will go north about the shaws
    And the deep ghylls that breed
Huge oaks and old, the which we hold
    No more than 'Sussex weed';
Or south where windy Piddinghoe's
    Begilded dolphin veers,
And black beside wide-bankèd Ouse
    Lie down our Sussex steers.

So to the land our hearts we give
    Till the sure magic strike,
And Memory, Use, and Love make live
    Us and our fields alike —
That deeper than our speech and thought,
    Beyond our reason's sway,
Clay of the pit whence we were wrought
    Yearns to its fellow-clay.

God gives all men all earth to love,
    But since man's heart is small,
Ordains for each one spot shall prove
    Beloved over all.
Each to his choice, and I rejoice
    The lot has fallen to me
In a fair ground — in a fair ground —
    Yea, Sussex by the sea!

RUDYARD KIPLING (1865–1936)

Cuttin' Rushes

OH, maybe it was yesterday, or fifty years ago!
Meself was risin' early on a day for cuttin' rushes,
Walkin' up the Brabla' burn, still the sun was low,
Now I'd hear the burn run an' then I'd hear the thrushes.

Young, still young! – an' drenchin' wet the grass,
Wet the golden honeysuckle hangin' sweetly down;
'Here, lad, here! will ye follow where I pass
An' find me cuttin' rushes on the mountain.'

Then was it only yesterday, or fifty years or so?
Rippin' round the bog pools high among the heather,
The hook it made her hand sore, she had to leave it go.
'Twas me that cut the rushes then for her to bind together.

Coome, dear, come! – an' back along the burn,
See the darlin' honeysuckle hangin' like a crown.
Quick, one kiss, – sure, there's someone at the turn,
'Oh, we're afther cuttin' rushes on the mountain.'

Yesterday, yesterday, or fifty years ago . . .
I waken out o' dreams when I hear the summer thrushes.
Oh, that's the Brabla' burn, I can hear it sing and flow,
For all that's fair, I'd sooner see a bunch o' green rushes.

Run, burn, run! can ye mind when we were young?
The honeysuckle hangs above, the pool is dark an' brown:
Sing, burn, sing! can ye mind the song ye sung
The day we cut the rushes on the mountain?

MOIRA O'NEILL (1864–1955)

Shoreham: Twilight Time

AND now the trembling light
Glimmers behind the little hills and corn,
Ling'ring as loth to part; yet part thou must
And though than open day far pleasing more
(Ere yet the fields and pearlèd cups of flowers
    Twinkle in the parting light;)
Thee night shall hide, sweet visionary gleam
That softly lookest through the rising dew;
    Till all like silver bright,
    The faithful witness, pure and white,
    Shall look o'er yonder grassy hill,
    At this village, safe and still.
    All is safe and all is still,
    Save what noise the watch-dog makes
    Or the shrill cock the silence breaks.
    Now and then –
    And now and then –
    Hark! Once again,
    The wether's bell
    To us doth tell
Some little stirring in the fold.
Methinks the ling'ring dying ray
Of twilight time, doth seem more fair,
And lights the soul up more than day
When wide-spread sultry sunshines are:
Yet all is right and all most fair,
For thou, dear God, has formèd all;
Thou deckest every little flower,
Thou girdest every planet ball,
And mark'st when sparrows fall.

SAMUEL PALMER (1805–1881)

From: *As You Like It*

Scene V Another part of the forest

Enter AMIENS, JAQUES, and others

Song

AMIENS   Under the greenwood tree
                  Who loves to lie with me,
                  And turn his merry note
                  Unto the sweet bird's throat,
Come hither, come hither, come hither.
                  Here shall he see
                  No enemy
But winter and rough weather.

                  All together here.

                  Who doth ambition shun,
                  And loves to live i' th' sun,
                  Seeking the food he eats,
                  And pleas'd with what he gets,
Come hither, come hither, come hither.
                  Here shall he see
                  No enemy
But winter and rough weather.
JAQUES   If it do come to pass
                  That any man turn ass,
                  Leaving his wealth and ease
                  A stubborn will to please,
Ducdame, ducdame, ducdame;
                  Here shall he see
                  Gross fools as he,
An if he will come to me.

WILLIAM SHAKESPEARE (1564–1616)

The Vagabond

To an air of Schubert

GIVE to me the life I love,
  Let the lave go by me,
Give the jolly heaven above
  And the byway nigh me.
Bed in the bush with stars to see,
  Bread I dip in the river –
There's the life for a man like me,
  There's the life for ever.

Let the blow fall soon or late,
  Let what will be o'er me;
Give the face of earth around
  And the road before me.
Wealth I seek not, hope nor love,
  Nor a friend to know me;
All I seek, the heaven above
  And the road below me.

Or let autumn fall on me
  Where afield I linger,
Silencing the bird on tree,
  Biting the blue finger.
White as meal the frosty field –
  Warm the fireside haven –
Not to autumn will I yield,
  Not to winter even!

Let the blow fall soon or late.
  Let what will be o'er me;
Give the face of earth around
  And the road before me.
Wealth I ask not, hope nor love,
  Nor a friend to know me;
All I ask, the heaven above
  And the road below me.

ROBERT LOUIS STEVENSON (1850–1894)

The Glory

THE glory of the beauty of the morning, –
The cuckoo crying over the untouched dew;
The blackbird that has found it; and the dove
That tempts me on to something sweeter than love;
White clouds ranged even and fair as new-mown hay;
The heat, the stir, the sublime vacancy
Of sky and meadow and forest and my own heart: –
The glory invites me, yet it leaves me scorning
All I can ever do, all I can be,
Beside the lovely of motion, shape, and hue,
The happiness I fancy fit to dwell
In beauty's presence. Shall I now this day
Begin to seek as far as heaven, as hell,
Wisdom or strength to match this beauty, start
And tread the pale dust pitted with small dark drops,
In hope to find whatever it is I seek,
Hearkening to short-lived happy-seeming things
That we know naught of, in the hazel copse?
Or must I be content with discontent
As larks and swallows are perhaps with wings?
And shall I ask at the day's end once more
What beauty is, and what I can have meant
By happiness? And shall I let all go,
Glad, weary, or both? Or shall I perhaps know
That I was happy oft and oft before,
Awhile forgetting how I am fast pent,
How dreary-swift, with naught to travel to,
Is Time? I cannot bite the day to the core.

EDWARD THOMAS (1878–1917)

From: *The Old Cumberland Beggar*

> . . . SHE who tends
> The toll-gate, when in summer at her door
> She turns her wheel, if on the road she sees
> The aged Beggar coming, quits her work,
> And lifts the latch for him that he may pass.
> The post-boy, when his rattling wheels o'ertake
> The aged Beggar in the woody lane,
> Shouts to him from behind; and, if thus warned
> The old Man does not change his course, the boy
> Turns with less noisy wheels to the roadside,
> And passes gently by — without a curse
> Upon his lips, or anger in his heart.
> He travels on, a solitary Man;
> His age has no companion. On the ground
> His eyes are turned, and, as he moves along,
> They move along the ground; and evermore,
> Instead of common and habitual sight
> Of fields with rural works, of hill and dale,
> And the blue sky, one little span of earth
> Is all his prospect. Thus, from day to day,
> Bow-bent, his eyes for ever on the ground,
> He plies his weary journey; seeing still,
> And seldom knowing that he sees, some straw,
> Some scattered leaf, or marks which, in one track,
> The nails of cart or chariot-wheel have left
> Impressed on the white road, — in the same line,
> At distance still the same. Poor Traveller!
> His staff trails with him; scarcely do his feet
> Distub the summer dust; he is so still
> In look and motion, that the cottage curs,
> Ere he have passed the door, will turn away,
> Weary of barking at him. Boys and girls,
> The vacant and the busy, maids and youths,
> And urchins newly breeched — all pass him by;
> Him even the slow-paced wagon leaves behind.

WILLIAM WORDSWORTH (1770–1850)

INDEX OF POETS

Index of First Lines

ACKNOWLEDGEMENTS

Permission to use copyright material is gratefully acknowledged to the following:

John Murray (Publishers) Ltd for *Middlesex* by Sir John Betjeman from *Collected Poems*; Peters Fraser & Dunlop Group Ltd for *Forefathers* by Edmund Blunden; Richard Gordon Lancelyn Green as Literary Executor for *The Ironfounders and Others* by Gordon Bottomley; Curtis Brown and John Farquharson on behalf of the copyright holder Mr Eric Robinson for *Hares at Play, Blackbird* and *August* by John Clare; Emmet M. Greene, Executor of the Estate of Padraic Colum for *An Old Woman of the Roads* by Padraic Colum from *Poems* published by Macmillan Inc.; Bantam Press, a division of Transworld Publishers Ltd, for *My Land* © Catherine Cookson 1988 from *Let Me Make Myself Plain*; The Literary Trustees of Walter de la Mare and the Society of Authors as their representative for *All That's Past* by Walter de la Mare; Faber and Faber (Publishers) Ltd for *Landscapes* by T. S. Eliot from *Collected Poems*; Patrick W. H. Harvey for *Ducks* by F. W. Harvey; David Higham Associates Limited for *Song at the Beginning of Autumn* by Elizabeth Jennings from *Collected Poems* published by Macmillan Inc.; André Deutsch Ltd for *April Rise* by Laurie Lee from *Selected Poems*; The Society of Authors as the literary representatives of the Estate of John Masefield for *Up On the Downs*, and *The West Wind* by John Masefield; Monro Pennefather and Co., Solicitors on behalf of the Estate of Sir Arthur Quiller-Couch for *Upon Eckington Bridge, River Avon* by Sir Arthur Quiller-Couch; J. M. Dent & Sons Ltd for *The Leaf Burners* by Ernest Rhys; David Higham Associates Limited for *Fern Hill* by Dylan Thomas from *The Poems* published by J. M. Dent & Sons Ltd; David Higham Associates Limited for *Prothalamion* by Francis Brett Young; the Trustees of the Wallace Collection for *The Swing* by Jean-Honoré Fragonard; His Grace the Duke of Rutland, Belvoir Castle/Bridgeman Art Library, London for *The Woodcutter's House* by Thomas Gainsborough; and the Bridgeman Art Library, London for supplying all the other paintings.

Whilst every effort has been made to trace all copyright holders the publishers apologise to any holders not acknowledged.